Homes with

Curb Appeal

103 Home Plans...
stylish exteriors & amazing interiors

Frank Betz

Introduction

Progress and innovation have changed the world we live in. Technology has launched us into a new level that has brought about countless advantages to our communities, but coupled with it comes a faster-paced lifestyle. It leaves us longing for a peaceful place to refuel at the end of the day where things are simpler and slower. We all need a place where we can retreat from the commotion to a spot that is safer, quieter and unhurried. This is the place we call "*Home.*"

No single definition will match another, for "home" means something unique and different to everyone. It might entail the picturesque, storybook look of a cozy Cottage. Some prefer the rustic, earthy components of a Craftsman-style home. Others imagine the time-honored detail of an Old World façade. Yet others dream of the sweeping front porch of a Country design. Our individual preferences are diverse, coming from varying lifestyles and geographies. But essentially, it all means the same thing to each of us — security, comfort and certainty. A place that is yours and yours alone, the place where your heart is..."*Home.*"

Enjoy your journey through this fine collection of designs. In it, we hope you will find your own particular and satisfying version of "*Home.*"

Table of Contents

Left | A façade of clapboard siding with board-and-batten shutters is ageless and classic, recalling the simplicity of yesterday's neighborhood.

Above Left | Accent pieces comprised of deep-toned woods emphasize the rich hardwood floors in the foyer.

Above Middle | Sleek bowl-style sinks set in granite countertops combine contemporary with tradition in the master bath.

Above Right | A white, coffered ceiling with hearty wheat-colored inlaid tones canopies the kitchen and breakfast room.

A DESIGNS DIRECT PUBLISHING BOOK

presented by

FRANK BETZ ASSOCIATES INC.

Betz Publishing, LLC.
2401 Lake Park Drive, Suite 250
Smyrna, GA 30080
888.717.3003 | www.homeswithcurbappeal.com

Floor plans and elevations are subject to change. Floor
plan dimensions are approximate. Consult working
drawings for actual dimensions and information.
Elevations are artists' conceptions.

Frank Betz – *President*

Laura Segers – *Editor-in-Chief*

Russell Moody – *Editor*

Martha Stalvey – *Editor*

Allen Bennetts – *Illustrator*

Joshua Thomas – *Art Director*

Contributing Writer – Sarah Hockman

Contributing Photographers – Happy
Terrebone/Happy Terrebone Photography,
Visual Solutions, Bryan Willy/Bryan
Willy Photography, Homestore Plans & Publications

Prepress services by DMG Inc., Atlanta
Printed by Toppan Printing Company, Hong Kong

ISBN   1 - 9 3 2 5 5 3 - 0 8 - 8

First Printing, January 2005

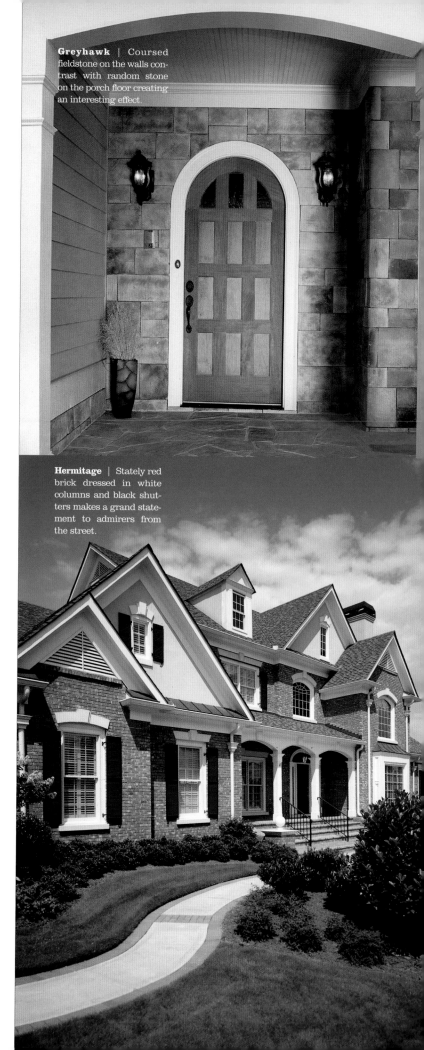

Greyhawk | Coursed fieldstone on the walls contrast with random stone on the porch floor creating an interesting effect.

Hermitage | Stately red brick dressed in white columns and black shutters makes a grand statement to admirers from the street.

Fairfield | Subdued earth tones on this traditional elevation blend well with the natural environment.

Flanagan | An eye-catching two-story stucco turret and white balusters accent red brick to create an original and interesting façade.

Gastonia | Board and batten shutters offer a casually elegant element to this traditional brick and siding façade.

Right - Hastings | The use of color, fabrics and furnishings allow homeowners to tailor their interior spaces to accommodate and recognize their ethnicity.

Far Right - Hastings | Contrasting reds and yellows tastefully come together to create an energetic, yet comfortable living room.

Frank Betz

Design Philosophy

We live in an ever-changing world, where the needs of homeowners change as their lifestyles do. With the hurriedness of everyday life, we recognize that the home should be a place where life simplifies and slows down. Focus has returned to the family, and so as residential designers our focus is to create homes that serve their residents in day-to-day living. Functional room arrangements are our priority. Practicality and purpose are the key elements that drive our thoughts and creativity as we begin crafting each design.

Keeping rooms serve as cozy extensions of the kitchen, expanding this space where we know family and friends tend to congregate. Often lit by a fireplace or bright and sunny with many windows, these spaces give families that casual and comfortable place to reconnect.

Raised rooms on the second floor have grown in popularity to be used as family recreation rooms or children's retreats. This common-sense design method utilizes the upper floor space that was once occupied by the two-story great room, providing homeowners with maximum square footage while still offering volume ceilings in the main - level family room.

Mudrooms and message centers are the small spaces that keep homes organized and tidy. The shedding of shoes, coats and backpacks is perfectly fine when there is a designated space for it. Family notes, daily mail and other household paperwork have their place in today's message centers. Often incorporated in or around the kitchen, these handy elements bring manageability to the stresses of daily life.

The opulent façade of the 80s is being replaced with a warmer, more casual one. Beauty is now being created by blending textures and colors to create eye-catching elevations. The availability of hybrid, low-maintenance materials created from cement fiber has re-launched the popularity of lap siding and shake. The use of these products has taken the exterior back to a warmer, more textured combination of materials, creating congeniality and casual elegance. Cupolas and carriage doors have transformed the garage from a single-purpose parking space to an attractive design element that enhances the curb appeal of the home.

Indeed, the necessities of the family-centered home are kinetic – a constantly changing set of priorities. As designers, we commit ourselves to a constant awareness of the needs of our customers. Our steady goal is to continue to create homes that are sensitive to hurried lifestyles, yet incorporate elements that simplify daily life. Our willingness to redefine "functional" and "practical" based on our changing world reflects our loyalty to today's family. It is with pride that we present this stunning assortment of our newest designs, created with you in mind. ■

Top Left - Randolph Place Time-honored design elements like a sweeping front porch and gabled roofline take passers-by for a walk down memory lane.

Top Right - Hastings | A cook - top island, stainless steel appliances and built-in shelving make the kitchen a state-of-the-art center point of the home.

Right - Hastings | Golden sheers highlight each window while still allowing plenty of natural light to illuminate the living space.

Right - Wilshire | A cheery white window box sits between bold black shutters to add and element of warmth to any façade.

Far Right - Carmel | Battered columns and eave brackets give the Craftsman appeal that has regained its popularity in today's neighborhoods.

Curb Appeal

Design Elements

The curb appeal of a home – the statement it makes from the street – sends a message to guests and passers-by. It communicates our personal style to the world around us. From clean-lined modern homes to multidimensional gabled looks, each home adds an element of individuality to the streetscape. Whether it is an assertion of formality or a declaration of casual sophistication, each home has a unique personality based on its architectural style. Four time-honored design varieties are covered in this collection: Cottage, Craftsman, Country and Old World — each with individual design elements that classify it as such. Design techniques borrowed from the past combine with up-to-date details and trends to create the façades that define the neighborhoods of today.

The Cottage - style design has an unmistakable charm that is felt from the street. It is a gracefully modest style that makes everyone feel welcome. Its unassuming casual elegance visually defines what "home" should mean. Front porches adorn many Cottage exteriors, always creating a friendly and comfortable environment. Masonry accents – such as fieldstone and brick – add a warmth and charm to front elevations. Board-and-batten shutters have renewed a nostalgic flare in the Cottage design. Once upon a time, shutters were purely functional providing safety from nature's elements. But the shutter has evolved into a decorative frame that accents the window and makes it a decorative element on the exterior of the home. Cozy details, such as copper accents and arbor - covered garage entries, give Cottage homes the established, timeless appeal

that so many homeowners long for. The Cottage style has an overall congeniality that is difficult to match and welcomed in any neighborhood.

Revived from the early 1900s the Craftsman design is regaining popularity. It possesses an understated beauty that was appealing to the people of that era, who were tiring of the formal Victorian style that had dominated in prior years. Today's Craftsman home borrows its style from the low-gabled bungalows that were constructed then, but adds some 21st-century charm with a warm and casual blend of exterior materials. While some homes still feature the simple use of lap siding for their exterior, others are combining cedar shake and stone to bring dimension and variety to the façade. Deep front porches are supported by pedestal-like battered columns. Eave brackets add simple ornamentation to the elevation, providing subtle decoration while maintaining architectural simplicity. Large, forward - facing gables create a clean-lined, down-to-earth impression from the street. Timber accents in the gables add wholesome detail to these pedestrian - friendly designs. The allure of the Craftsman home is as popular as ever, with rustic simplicity being its primary appeal.

Country-style homes are as pure and genuine as anything else that shares the name. Country cooking, country music, country living, a drive in the country — all of these are as American as apple pie. Country homes are warm and welcoming. They take us to a time when front - porch rocking chairs were worn from overuse. The Country-style home is today's revival of yesterday's farmhouse, updated into one- and two-story designs. Massive front porches are made deep enough for swings and rocking chairs. Cheery dormers give a friendly salutation to visitors and onlookers. Traditional combinations of lap siding and brick generate an age-old, but new - again simplicity that has regained fame in today's market. Once used to predict the weather, cupolas now sit sturdily atop garages to create a reminiscent decorative appeal. With countless details borrowed from the American past, country designs are a regeneration of yesteryear's family home.

European architecture inspires the Old World design. Homes of this style would be as commonly seen in a French village as they would an American neighborhood. Warm and earthy exterior materials create striking façades. Stucco and fieldstone or stately brick team up to create a sturdy, historic look. Old World designs tend toward opulence versus informality, with strong and

Above Far Right - Randolph Place | A rocking-chair front porch provides a connection to the outdoors, giving its homeowner a tranquil spot to unwind or converse with neighbors.

Above Right - Greyhawk | Casual furniture and shabby - chic accent pieces create a room where it's perfectly okay to kick up your feet.

Above - Moody Residence Soaring white columns and a covered side entrance give this façade a tasteful blend of casual and elegant living.

dignified exterior elevations. However, a more casual spin can be incorporated by turning to board-and-batten siding to bring a more relaxed flare to this style. Stone or stucco turrets create the feel of yesterday's European chateau. Alcove entries add a formal charm, usually arched in shape to mirror the historic architectural style. Old World designs – as grand and dignified as they are — remain rich in charisma and charm.

While these distinctive styles share some accent techniques and crossover in exterior materials, their overall appeal is unique and original. Each design draws from a different period of our history and sends its own message to the curb that reflects that era. They share a common purpose of presenting warmth and charm to our 21st-century neighborhoods – a good-natured, wholesome greeting to friends and family. Each design represents a personality shared with its homeowner, giving others a glimpse into personal style. From casual and comfortable to stately and strong, these styles share a special charisma that adds a friendly and hospitable element to our community. ▪

Above Left - Glenleigh | Stacked stone and cedar shakes subtly accent this traditional façade adding texture and congeniality to its curb appeal.

Right - Finley | Stark white stucco accents and a leaded - glass door make a strong and stately first impression from the street.

Making the Right

Home Plan Choice

Choosing your dream home is perhaps one of the most important decisions you can make. It is the space that not only needs to interact well with the style of your family, but also be the comfortable place to land in today's fast-paced world. It is the arena where your most important daily activities will take place – from helping with homework to hosting holiday dinners.

The process of choosing your home plan can seem like an overwhelming task with so many choices to make. There are charming Cottages, nostalgic Old World designs, simplistic Craftsman styles, and comfortable Country homes. There are open, flowing floor plans and more compartmented, private ones. From conservative to grand, the options are truly endless in the quest for your dream home.

THE PROCESS OF CHOOSING YOUR HOME CAN BE SIMPLIFIED BY REVIEWING YOUR VALUES AND ANALYZING YOUR LIFESTYLE. START WITH A FEW GENERAL QUESTIONS:

How much space do I want or need?

While some homeowners are on the quest for larger, more spacious rooms, others desire more conservatively sized, quainter spaces. Some homes will accommodate growing families, while others are more suited for empty - nesters and retirees.

What footprint dimensions will fit properly on my lot?

Lot shapes and sizes often dictate the size and shape of the structure that is built on it. Consider how much yard space you want left over. Some prefer an easier maintained small area, while those with children are likely to desire ample play space in their yards.

Does this space need to be child - friendly?

The family-friendly home design can differ greatly from the one that is more geared toward adult interaction. Families tend to be drawn to bedrooms tucked away on an upper level, while an entertainer may prefer that her home's square footage is spent on intertwining gathering spots.

Do I want one-level living or two stories?

One-level living is popular due in great part to its easy access to all living places. If stairs are seen as a burden, a ranch might just be the choice for you. A second floor often houses children's bedrooms and baths, recreation rooms or children's retreats, master suites, and bonus space. Generally, family time is dedicated to the main floor in the kitchen, keeping room or family room, while the private areas are situated on the upper floor.

What exterior style best suits my taste?

While the floor plan of the home is key to your lifestyle activities, everyone has a certain "look" that comes to mind when picturing their dream home. Some may seek a stately, formal curb appeal, while others are more drawn to simple, casual designs. A common misconception is that floor plan options are limited by your choice of exterior style, but that's simply not true. There are countless floor plans that have been coupled with each style. Your options are endless.

If you're able to answer the few general questions mentioned before, you're well on your way to finding the plan that's right for you and your family. Although you've narrowed the search, you may still be left with many, many options. It's time now to address some specifics about your day-to-day lifestyle that will help zero in on the perfect home.

Think about your day. How many people does your home need to accommodate? Are you a telecommuter who needs a home office? Do you spend your day caring for children? Are you a frequent entertainer? What type of room arrangements best suit your lifestyle – more formal living room/dining room arrangements or more casual gathering spaces such as recreation rooms and keeping rooms? Where do you want your laundry facilities?

All of these factors dictate the layout of your home. Clearly, larger families need more space. They need bedrooms to accommodate all family members, mealtime gathering spots, recreation areas and perhaps study space for children. Additional bathrooms are often a plus, providing privacy and convenience for all family members.

Telecommuting is a growing trend in our nation. Even those households that don't telecommute, however, still request a home office—a place where computers, printers and fax machines have a home. The daily chore of keeping up with managing the household is much easier when there's a dedicated space from which to work.

Entertainers often prefer more open, flowing designs, where each main living space gently connects to the next offering easy access from room to room. If you're the party-thrower on the block, you may want to consider a design with this type of arrangement. Whether you prefer one story, two stories, a main - level master or a multilevel, you'll be able to find an open, spacious layout in many home plans.

While the location of the laundry room may seem insignificant to some, it is very important to the person responsible for this chore. If you're choosing a two-story design, you may find more convenience in an upstairs location, with easy access to the bedrooms. If one-story designs suit you the best, you may find that a laundry room located near the garage doubling as a mudroom will have great fringe benefits.

There is a home plan for everyone. Review your needs and preferences. Analyze your daily activities. Think back to the times when you found yourself saying, "Wouldn't it be nice if….?" about your current home or "In my next house I'd want…". Whatever your lifestyle and personal taste dictate, there is a perfect home plan for you. ▪

Maple Grove Cottage (pages 24 to 25) Deep front porches are made to be spaces that are shared by family and friends — with or without fur.

Right | Window boxes bursting with red flowers and green ivy creeping over the garage add a cheery charm and character to the street view of this home.

Visit www.homeswithcurbappeal.com for complete details on the Maple Grove Cottage.

Cottages

CHOOSING A COTTAGE-STYLE HOME IS MORE THAN

opting for a specific look – it's electing a way of life. This style is for those who prefer contentment and tradition over chic and passing trends. It's not about keeping up with the Jones', but rather having them to dinner. The Cottage home is as inviting on the inside as it is from the street.

Cottage style might mean the careful placement of cozy fieldstone accents or cheery dormers in the roofline. Perhaps it means a charming front porch or a crackling fire in the keeping room. There are countless defining features that make a home a Cottage, but the key element is its graceful presentation from entry to exit. It is an unpretentious, yet casually elegant charm that makes every lucky visitor look forward to a quick return.

© Frank Betz Associates, Inc.

Daventry

Designer's Notes

Plan number: CAFB03-3868
PRICE CODE: **B**

Traditional elements combine with a cottage-like appeal to create an inviting façade on the Daventry. This two-story design is eye-catching with a front porch deep enough to accommodate any rocking chair! Lattice accents on the columns make this front elevation even more interesting. Inside, the entire first level is dedicated solely to common living spaces, making this an ideal design for those who like to entertain. A coat closet and powder room are situated just inside the front door. The master suite has a beautiful tray ceiling and a nicely appointed master bath. Laundry facilities are nestled among the bedrooms, adding convenience to this household chore.

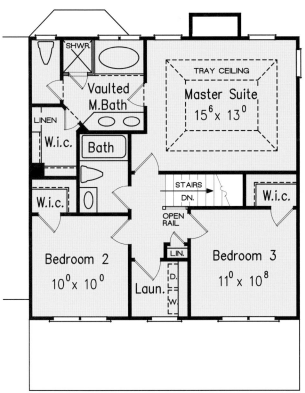

TRAY CEILING

Master Suite
15^6 x 13^0

SHWR.

Vaulted M.Bath

LINEN

W.i.c.

Bath

W.i.c.

STAIRS DN.

OPEN RAIL

W.i.c.

Bedroom 2
10^0 x 10^0

LIN.

Laun.

D.

W.

Bedroom 3
11^0 x 10^8

second floor

rear elevation

Bedrooms: 3

Baths: 2.5

Width: 49'-0"

Depth: 37'-8"

Main Level: 805 sq ft

Second Level: 758 sq ft

Living Area: 1563 sq ft

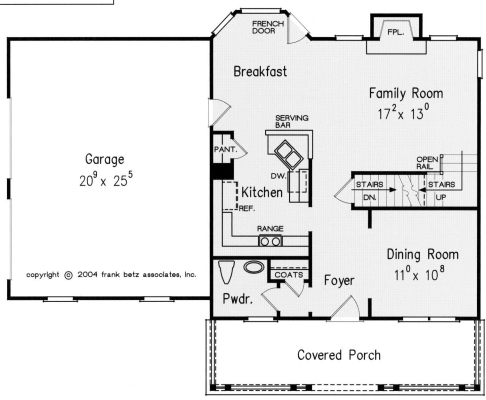

FRENCH DOOR

FPL.

Breakfast

Family Room
17^2 x 13^0

SERVING BAR

PANT.

DW.

Kitchen

REF.

RANGE

OPEN RAIL

STAIRS DN.

STAIRS UP

copyright © 2004 frank betz associates, inc.

Garage
20^9 x 25^5

COATS

PWDR.

Foyer

Dining Room
11^0 x 10^8

Covered Porch

first floor

Musgrave

Designer's Notes

Plan number: CAFB03-3526
PRICE CODE: **D**

Stepping up from your starter? The Musgrave might be just what you're looking for! A main - floor bedroom is the ideal location for a guest suite with direct access to a full bath. Telecommuters may opt to use this space as a home office. The second - floor bedrooms have walk-in closets and share a divided bath. A computer nook has been thoughtfully incorporated into the upper level giving children a private and convenient homework station. The optional bonus space could be easily finished to create a playroom, fitness area or crafting room for Mom.

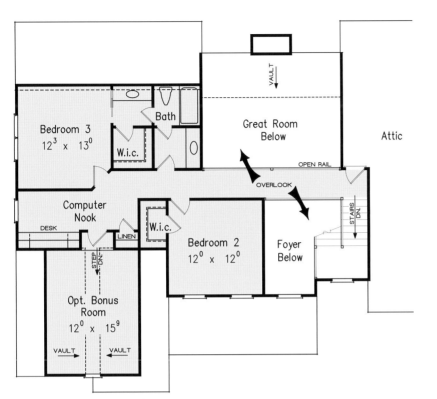

Bedroom 3
12^3 x 13^0

Bath

W.i.c.

Great Room
Below

VAULT

Attic

OPEN RAIL

OVERLOOK

STAIRS DN.

Computer
Nook

DESK

LINEN

W.i.c.

STEP DN.

Bedroom 2
12^0 x 12^0

Foyer
Below

Opt. Bonus
Room
12^0 x 15^9

VAULT

VAULT

second floor

rear elevation

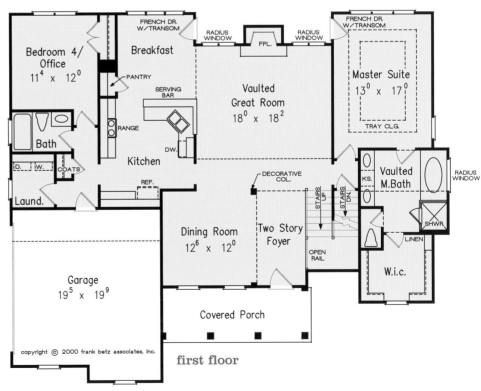

Bedroom 4/
Office
11^4 x 12^0

FRENCH DR.
W/TRANSOM

Breakfast

RADIUS
WINDOW

FPL.

RADIUS
WINDOW

FRENCH DR.
W/TRANSOM

Master Suite
13^0 x 17^0

PANTRY

SERVING
BAR

Vaulted
Great Room
18^0 x 18^2

TRAY CLG.

RANGE

DW.

Bath

D. W.

COATS

Kitchen

REF.

DECORATIVE
COL.

KS.

Vaulted
M.Bath

RADIUS
WINDOW

Laund.

SHWR.

LINEN

Dining Room
12^6 x 12^0

STAIRS UP

STAIRS DN.

Two Story
Foyer

OPEN
RAIL

W.i.c.

Garage
19^5 x 19^9

Covered Porch

copyright © 2000 frank betz associates, inc.

first floor

Bedrooms: 4

Baths: 3

Width: 58'-0"

Depth: 47'-0"

Main Level: 1720 sq ft

Second Level: 724 sq ft

Living Area: 2444 sq ft

Opt. Bonus Room: 212 sq ft

Graves Spring

Designer's Notes

Plan number: CAFB03-3852
PRICE CODE: **F**

From the Southern Living Design Collection™ – A warm, welcoming façade and thoughtful design make this "house" a "home." Timber-accented gables and board-and-batten shutters give the Graves Spring phenomenal curb appeal. Inside, a well-designed floor plan has been created for day-to-day living. The great room is accented with a coffered ceiling for a dramatic effect. A covered side entrance takes traffic through a mudroom, keeping shoes and coats where they belong. A main-floor guest room also makes the perfect home office for today's busy mom or telecommuter. Upstairs, a family recreation area is situated among three bedrooms, making a great area for playing games, watching television or doing homework.

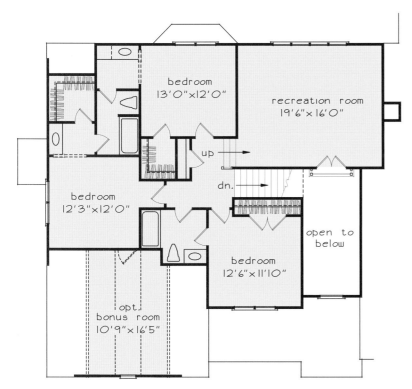

bedroom
13'0"×12'0"

recreation room
19'6"×16'0"

up

dn.

bedroom
12'3"×12'0"

open to
below

bedroom
12'6"×11'10"

opt.
bonus room
10'9"×16'5"

second floor

rear elevation

deck

master bedroom
14'9"×20'0"

kitchen
13'5"×13'5"

breakfast
12'0"×13'6"

great room
19'6"×16'0"

dn.

up

dining
12'6"×14'2"

foyer

garage
21'5"× 23'3"

bedroom
12'2"×14'3"

covered porch

copyright © 2003 frank betz associates, inc.

first floor

Bedrooms: 5

Baths: 4

Width: 67'-0"

Depth: 54'-6"

Main Level: 2096 sq ft

Second Level: 1184 sq ft

Living Area: 3280 sq ft

Opt. Bonus Room: 187 sq ft

© Frank Betz Associates, Inc.

Sutcliffe

Designer's Notes

Plan number: CAFB03-3634
PRICE CODE: **F**

A sweeping front porch against a façade of cedar shakes makes an attention-grabbing exterior on the Sutcliffe design. Its floor plan was designed with today's growing family in mind, giving the lucky homeowner many extras that can be hard to find today. Curl up with a good book in the window seat of the private sitting area in the master suite. Decorative columns "define" this space to create a peaceful haven for the homeowner. A guest bedroom with its own private bath is designed into the main floor, tucked away off the family room for privacy. The kitchen is an entertainer's dream, with a large prep island, open layout and decorative shelving.

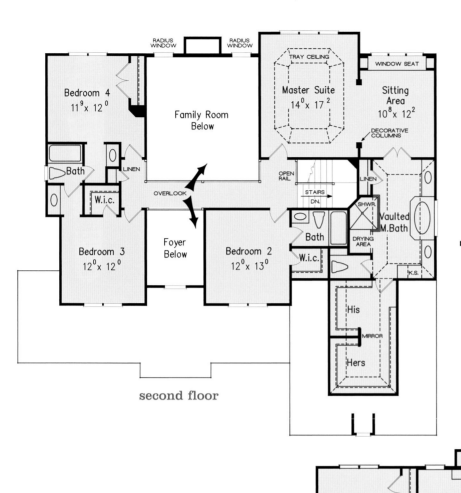

RADIUS WINDOW   RADIUS WINDOW

Bedroom 4
11⁹ x 12⁰

Family Room
Below

TRAY CEILING

Master Suite
14⁰ x 17²

WINDOW SEAT

Sitting
Area
10⁸ x 12²

Bath

LINEN

OVERLOOK

W.i.c.

Bedroom 3
12⁰ x 12⁰

Foyer
Below

Bedroom 2
12⁰ x 13⁰

OPEN RAIL

STAIRS DN.

DECORATIVE COLUMNS

LINEN

SHWR

Vaulted
M.Bath

Bath

DRYING AREA

W.i.c.

K.S.

His

MIRROR

Hers

second floor

rear elevation

FRENCH DOOR

FPL.

SHELVES

DW.

Guest Bedroom
11⁹ x 12⁰

Two Story
Family Room
16⁰ x 21⁰

Breakfast

ISLAND

SURFACE UNIT

Kitchen

OVEN

REF.

PANTRY

Bath

LINEN

COATS

Pwdr.

STAIRS UP

STAIRS DN.

Laund.

SINK

W.   D.

Study
12⁰ x 13⁰

FRENCH DOORS

Two Story
Foyer

Dining Room
13⁰ x 13⁰

Garage
20⁵ x 31⁰

Covered Porch

first floor

copyright © 2001 frank betz associates, inc.

Bedrooms: 5

Baths: 4.5

Width: 60'-0"

Depth: 56'-0"

Main Level: 1692 sq ft

Second Level: 1620 sq ft

Living Area: 3312 sq ft

© Frank Betz Associates, Inc.

rear elevation

Bedrooms: 3

Baths: 2

Width: 50'-4"

Depth: 49'-0"

Main Level: 1406 sq ft

Living Area: 1406 sq ft

Abbotts Pond

Designer's Notes

Plan number: CAFB03-3856
PRICE CODE: **C**

The Abbotts Pond is conservative in square footage and abundant in charisma. Board-and-batten siding and a covered front porch say, "Please, come in!"

From the foyer, a clear view to the back of the home makes this space feel roomy and welcoming. A covered back porch makes a tranquil evening retreat.

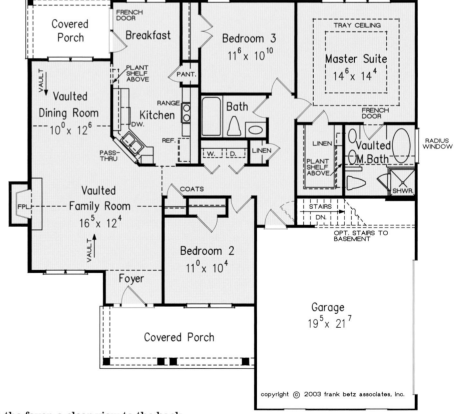

first floor

copyright © 2003 frank betz associates, inc.

© Frank Betz Associates, Inc.

rear elevation

Bedrooms: 3

Baths: 2

Width: 51'-0"

Depth: 51'-0"

Main Level: 1502 sq ft

Living Area: 1502 sq ft

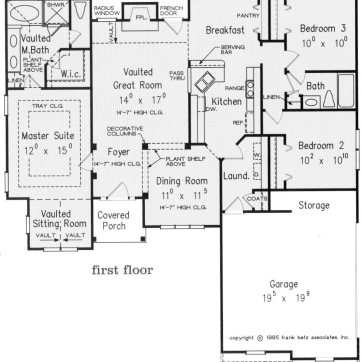

opt. basement stair location

first floor

Huntsville

Designer's Notes

Plan number: CAFB03-919

PRICE CODE: **C**

Large radius windows allow plenty of light to pour into the Huntsville design, creating a bright and cheery environment inside. The kitchen, breakfast area and great room are all easily accessible to each other, making family gatherings and parties fun and interactive. A coat closet and laundry room are strategically placed just off the garage, keeping coats and shoes in their place.

© Frank Betz Associates, Inc.

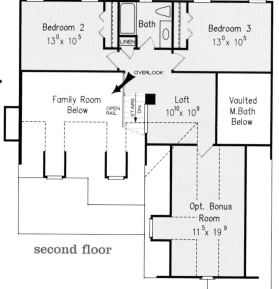

rear elevation

Bedrooms: 3

Baths: 2.5

Width: 42'-4"

Depth: 44'-0"

Main Level: 1012 sq ft

Second Level: 577 sq ft

Living Area: 1589 sq ft

Opt. Bonus Room: 253 sq ft

Culverhouse

Designer's Notes

Plan number: CAFB03-3827
PRICE CODE: **B**

The neat and cheery façade of the Culverhouse is a welcomed look on any street. A vaulted family room gently blends with the dining room and kitchen to generate a unified gathering spot for family and friends. Upstairs, two flexible spaces have been incorporated into the design — a loft and bonus room — to be used as homeowners wish.

second floor

first floor

copyright © 2003 frank betz associates, inc.

TO ORDER PLANS CALL TOLL FREE 888-717-3003

© Frank Betz Associates, Inc.

rear elevation

Bedrooms: 3

Baths: 2

Width: 53'-0"

Depth: 50'-6"

Main Level: 1591 sq ft

Living Area: 1591 sq ft

Forsythe

Designer's Notes

Plan number: CAFB03-3686

PRICE CODE: **B**

Shingles, brick and siding create a handsome blend of exterior materials for this classic ranch-style home. Vaulted ceilings enhance the public rooms of this flexible interior, invit-ing planned events as well as impromptu gatherings. Off the foyer are sleeping quarters that include a master suite with a vaulted bath, and two secondary bedrooms.

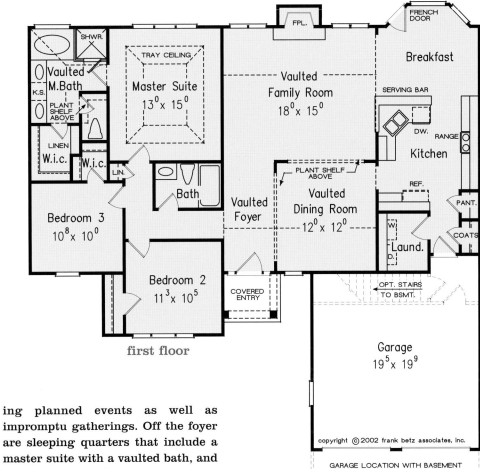

first floor

© Frank Betz Associates, Inc.

rear elevation

Bedrooms: 4

Baths: 3

Width: 54'-0"

Depth: 52'-0"

Main Level: 1694 sq ft

Living Area: 1694 sq ft

Opt. Second Floor: 588 sq ft

Greystone

Designer's Notes

Plan number: CAFB03-3875
PRICE CODE: **B**

The Greystone combines comfort with style to provide top-notch, one-level living. A decorative column creates an unobtrusive border that defines the dining room, making the entrance of the home feel open and spacious. Transom windows in the family room invite plenty of sunshine into the room, keeping this space bright and cheery.

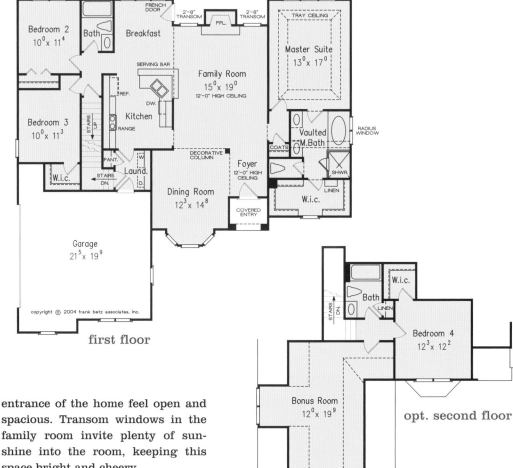

first floor

opt. second floor

© Frank Betz Associates, Inc.

rear elevation

Bedrooms: 3

Baths: 2

Width: 54'-0"

Depth: 59'-6"

Main Level: 1768 sq ft

Living Area: 1768 sq ft

Opt. Second Floor: 354 sq ft

Brookhollow

Designer's Notes

Plan number: CAFB03-3694
PRICE CODE: **C**

Copper window accents, brick and an arched covered entry come together to create a warm Brookhollow welcome for family and guests. The main living area is airy and unobtrusive, with decorative columns serving as the subtle border of the dining room. Radius windows on each side of the fireplace allow the natural light to pour into this living space.

first floor

opt. second floor

© Frank Betz Associates, Inc.

rear elevation

Bedrooms: 3

Baths: 2

Width: 54'-0"

Depth: 53'-0"

Main Level: 1795 sq ft

Living Area: 1795 sq ft

Opt. Bonus Room: 254 sq ft

Priceville

Designer's Notes

Plan number: CAFB03-1179
PRICE CODE: **C**

Sometimes it's the details that set one house apart from its counterparts. The Priceville showcases some of those added extras. Plant shelves, radius windows and decorative columns are tastefully placed throughout the home. French doors lead to the master bath, where highlights include a seated shower and his-and-her closets.

first floor

Vaulted M.Bath
KS.
SEAT
SHWR
His
Hers
FRENCH DOOR
Master Suite
15⁰ x 13⁰
TRAY CLG.
OPT. OPNG.
Living Room/ Sitting Room
11⁵ x 13⁶
COATS
Porch
Vaulted Foyer
15'-0" CLG. HT.
PLANT SHELF ABOVE
DECORATIVE COLS.
Vaulted Great Room
14⁰ x 17⁰
15'-0" CLG. HT.
RADIUS WINDOW
FPL.
RADIUS ABOVE
PLANT SHELF ABOVE
FRENCH DOOR
Breakfast
SERVING BAR
RANGE
DW.
REF.
Kitchen
PANTRY
W
Vaulted Dining Room
11² x 11²
15'-0" CLG. HT.
Laund.
COATS
W.i.c.
OPT. STAIRS DN. TO BSMT.
STAIRS UP
W.i.c.
LINEN
Bedroom 3
10⁰ x 10⁰
Bath
Bedroom 2
10⁰ x 12⁵
Garage
19⁵ x 20⁷

copyright © 1998 frank betz associates, inc.

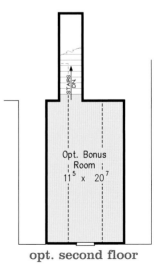

Opt. Bonus Room
11⁵ x 20⁷
STAIRS DN.

opt. second floor

© Frank Betz Associates, Inc.

Willow

Designer's Notes

Plan number: CAFB03-1085
PRICE CODE: **D**

This home uses its space wisely, with function in every corner. The master suite encompasses one entire side of the home, giving homeowners the privacy of being the only residents on the main floor. An optional bonus room is available on the second floor, offering homeowners endless possibilities for expansion to a playroom, exercise area or home office.

rear elevation

Bedrooms: 3

Baths: 2.5

Width: 52'-4"

Depth: 45'-10"

Main Level: 1382 sq ft

Second Level: 436 sq ft

Living Area: 1818 sq ft

Opt. Bonus Room: 298 sq ft

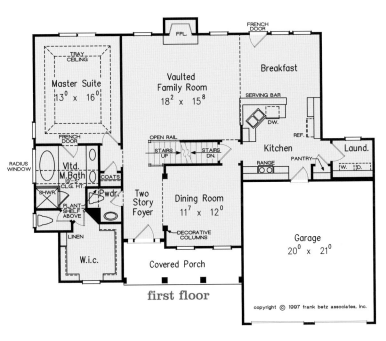

first floor

copyright © 1997 frank betz associates, inc.

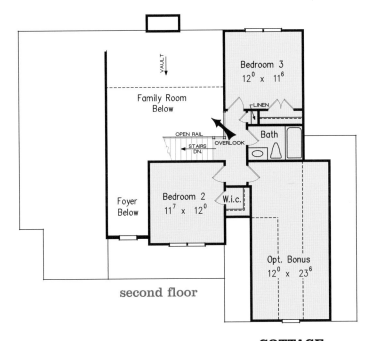

second floor

© Frank Betz Associates, Inc.

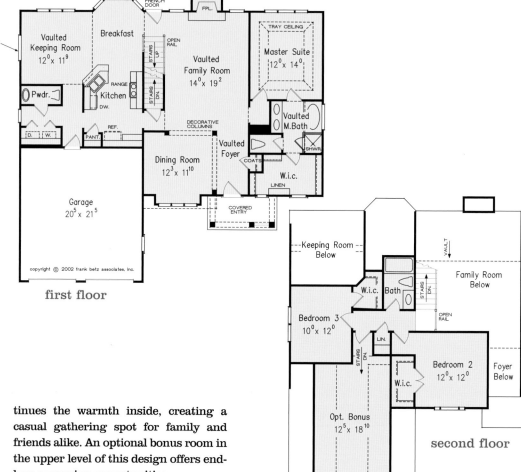

rear elevation

Bedrooms: 3

Baths: 2.5

Width: 51'-0"

Depth: 46'-4"

Main Level: 1397 sq ft

Second Level: 482 sq ft

Living Area: 1879 sq ft

Opt. Bonus Room: 267 sq ft

Glenallen

Designer's Notes

Plan number: CAFB03-3739
PRICE CODE: **C**

Brick and cedar shakes are accented with board-and-batten shutters to create a cottage-like façade that is welcomed in many neighborhoods today. A vaulted keeping room just off the kitchen con- tinues the warmth inside, creating a casual gathering spot for family and friends alike. An optional bonus room in the upper level of this design offers end- less expansion opportunities.

© Frank Betz Associates, Inc.

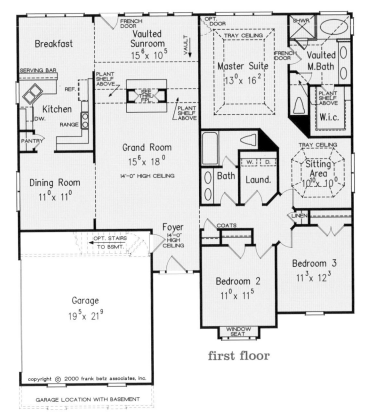

rear elevation

Bedrooms: 3

Baths: 2

Width: 50'-0"

Depth: 53'-0"

Main Level: 1902 sq ft

Living Area: 1902 sq ft

Newbern

Designer's Notes

Plan number: CAFB03-3548

PRICE CODE: **C**

The Newbern is one of those special designs that has a cozy and friendly feeling from the curb, as well as inside. Its most unique features are a see-through fireplace that adjoins the grand room and a vaulted sunroom. Another unique space in this design is a private sitting area in the master suite, accented with an octagonal tray ceiling. An optional door can be incorporated from the suite into the sunroom.

© Frank Betz Associates, Inc.

rear elevation

Bedrooms: 4

Baths: 3

Width: 56'-6"

Depth: 57'-6"

Main Level: 1915 sq ft

Living Area: 1915 sq ft

Birmingham

Designer's Notes

Plan number: CAFB03-1119
PRICE CODE: **C**

The Birmingham's brick - accented façade is simple and understated, with a friendly appeal that many home-owners seek in their search for a home. The kitchen, breakfast area and great room intertwine, creating easy access from one room to another. A fourth bedroom can be modified to a study or home office, perfect for the telecommuter.

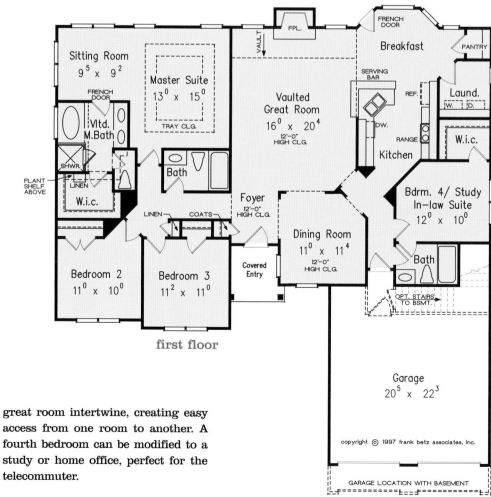

first floor

© Frank Betz Associates, Inc.

Brookhaven

Designer's Notes

Plan number: CAFB03-963
PRICE CODE: **E**

Artful exterior design leads to a carefully planned layout inside the Brookhaven. A bedroom on the main level has direct access to a bathing area, mak-ing this space an ideal guest room or home office. The upstairs bedrooms feature walk-in closets and share a bath with separate private lavatory areas.

rear elevation

Bedrooms: 4

Baths: 3

Width: 53'-0"

Depth: 47'-0"

Main Level: 1583 sq ft

Second Level: 543 sq ft

Living Area: 2126 sq ft

Opt. Bonus Room: 251 sq ft

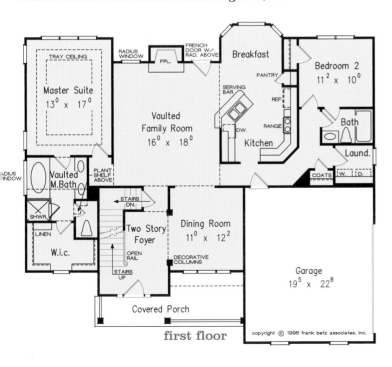

first floor

copyright © 1996 frank betz associates, inc.

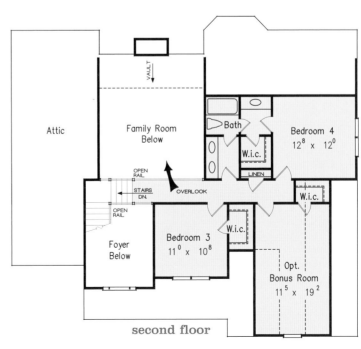

second floor

© Frank Betz Associates, Inc.

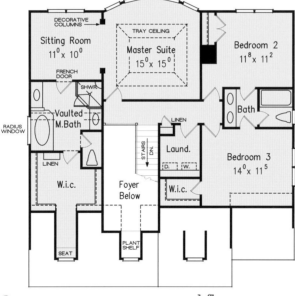

second floor

rear elevation

Bedrooms: 4

Baths: 3

Width: 41'-0"

Depth: 43'-0"

Main Level: 1042 sq ft

Second Level: 1150 sq ft

Living Area: 2192 sq ft

first floor

Kimball Bridge

Designer's Notes

Plan number: CAFB03-3696
PRICE CODE: **D**

This home has earned its cottage classification, with its cheery dormers, covered front porch and simple roofline. A bowed wall of windows in the family room creates a dramatic backdrop for the entire main living space, allowing plenty of sunshine to pour in. This feature is incorporated into the master suite upstairs, giving homeowners the same cheerful environment as downstairs.

© Frank Betz Associates, Inc.

Laurel Springs

Designer's Notes

Plan number: CAFB03-3854
PRICE CODE: **D**

Timber - accented gables and carriage doors team up to produce a cottage - style façade that is friendly and warm. Decorative columns create a promenade through the

rear elevation

foyer leading to the family room and kitchen area. The master suite enjoys the privacy of being the only bedroom on the main level of the home.

Bedrooms: 4

Baths: 3.5

Width: 51'-0"

Depth: 44'-4"

Main Level: 1381 sq ft

Lower Level: 820 sq ft

Living Area: 2201 sq ft

Opt. Second Floor: 331 sq ft

lower level

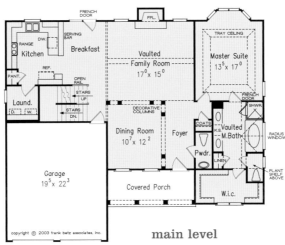

main level

copyright © 2003 frank betz associates, inc.

optional second floor

© Frank Betz Associates, Inc.

rear elevation

Bedrooms: 3

Baths: 2.5

Width: 54'-0"

Depth: 54'-6"

Main Level: 1784 sq ft

Second Level: 478 sq ft

Living Area: 2262 sq ft

Opt. Bonus Room: 336 sq ft

Ardsley

Designer's Notes

Plan number: CAFB03-3624
PRICE CODE: **D**

Nothing creates a cottage-like appeal better than a covered front porch, welcoming you in to make yourself at home. Just off the foyer, a study makes an ideal location for a home office which converts into a master suite sitting area, if you so choose. Special extras, such as the built-in message center and an optional bonus room, make this design a highly functional choice for today's busy family.

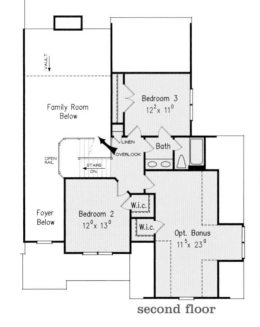

second floor

first floor

© Frank Betz Associates, Inc.

Hillsborough

Designer's Notes

Plan number: CAFB03-1022
PRICE CODE: **D**

The classic combination of brick and siding is emphasized by copper accents over the windows to create a warm and appealing façade on the Hillsborough. Entertainers will love the connected living and dining rooms, divided only by decorative columns, making traffic flow effortless from one room to the other.

rear elevation

Bedrooms:	4
Baths:	3
Width:	45'-0"
Depth:	43'-4"
Main Level:	1290 sq ft
Second Level:	985 sq ft
Living Area:	2275 sq ft
Opt. Bonus Room:	186 sq ft

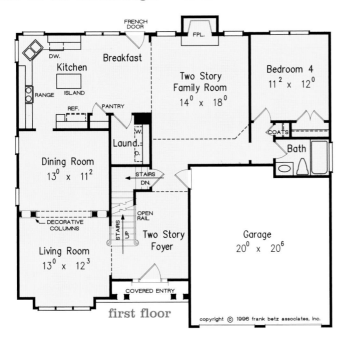

first floor

copyright © 1996 frank betz associates, inc.

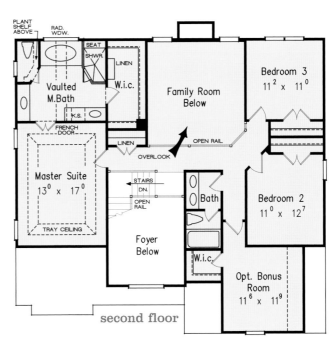

second floor

© Frank Betz Associates, Inc.

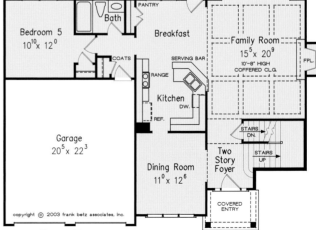

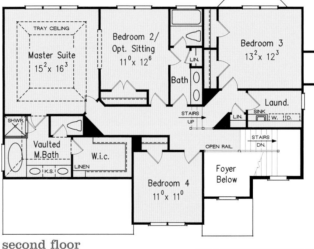

rear elevation

second floor

first floor

Bedrooms: 5

Baths: 3

Width: 50'-4"

Depth: 37'-9"

Main Level: 1108 sq ft

Second Level: 1253 sq ft

Living Area: 2361 sq ft

Glenbrooke

Designer's Notes

Plan number: CAFB03-3788
PRICE CODE: **D**

The Glenbrooke is a very smart design, giving the homeowners options on how they want to use their space. The bedroom on the main level of the home can remain as such, but can also make an ideal guest room or be easily converted into a home office. Another bedroom on the upper level can also be a generous sitting area adjoining the master suite.

© Frank Betz Associates, Inc.

rear elevation

Bedrooms: 3

Baths: 2.5

Width: 41'-4"

Depth: 51'-0"

Main Level: 1120 sq ft

Second Level: 1250 sq ft

Living Area: 2370 sq ft

second floor

first floor

Millstone Cottage

Designer's Notes

Plan number: CAFB03-3786
PRICE CODE: **D**

Carriage doors, fieldstone accents, board-and-batten shutters — what creates a cottage-like appeal more than this awesome combination? A generously sized family room is canopied by a coffered ceiling, creating a dramatic first impression. The kitchen and breakfast areas are adjoined by a keeping room overlooking the backyard. Covered porches are accessed from the breakfast area and the master suite.

© Frank Betz Associates, Inc.

rear elevation

Bedrooms: 4

Baths: 2.5

Width: 50'-0"

Depth: 42'-6"

Main Level: 1033 sq ft

Second Level: 1359 sq ft

Living Area: 2392 sq ft

Chestnut Springs

Designer's Notes

Plan number: CAFB03-3621
PRICE CODE: **D**

Timeless simplicity sums up the Chestnut Springs with its covered front porch and carriage garage doors. The main floor of this design is dedicated exclusively to common living areas, giving extra privacy to the bedrooms upstairs. A large island in the kitchen aids in meal preparation.

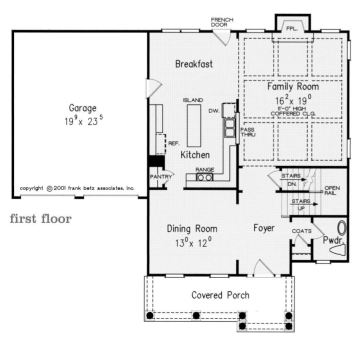

first floor

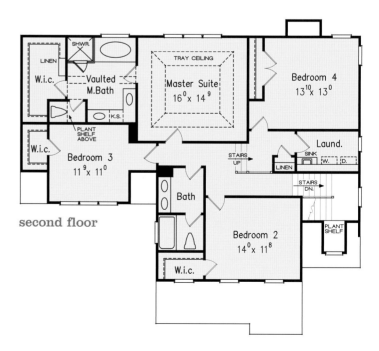

second floor

© Frank Betz Associates, Inc.

rear elevation

Bedrooms: 4

Baths: 3.5

Width: 61'-6"

Depth: 67'-6"

Main Level: 2487 sq ft

Living Area: 2487 sq ft

Opt. Second Floor: 306 sq ft

Rankins

Designer's Notes

Plan number: CAFB03-3829

PRICE CODE: **D**

The Rankins was created for that home-owner who is looking for a functional, well-planned design with upscale amenities that make a house a home. The core of the home is the family room that is made extra special with coffered ceilings and built-in cabinetry. The master suite is adorned with a seated shower, a step-up soaking tub and an optional private sitting area.

optional second floor

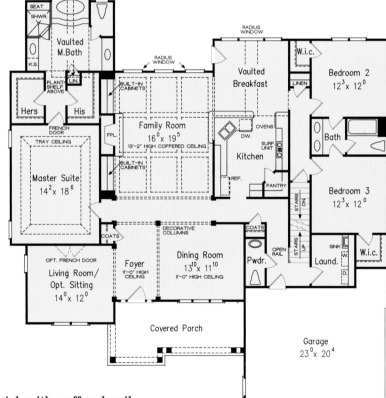

first floor

© Frank Betz Associates, Inc.

rear elevation

Bedrooms: 5

Baths: 4

Width: 41'-0"

Depth: 66'-0"

Main Level: 1355 sq ft

Second Level: 1347 sq ft

Living Area: 2702 sq ft

Opt. Bonus Room: 285 sq ft

Dominion

Designer's Notes

Plan number: CAFB03-3754
PRICE CODE: **F**

A true "cottage," this design beckons you in to see more with its cozy field-stone and dormer - accented exterior. The kitchen overlooks a keeping room that is nestled on the back of the home with great views to the backyard. A coffered ceiling and transom windows in the family room make this space bright and comfortable. An optional bonus room has interesting angles with dormers and window seats.

second floor

Master Suite 13⁵ x 17⁰

Sitting Area 8⁰ x 12⁰

Bath

Bedroom 2 13⁰ x 12⁹

Vaulted M.Bath

Foyer Below

W.i.c.

Bedroom 3 11⁰ x 13²

Laund.

Bath

Opt. Bonus/ Bedroom 5 12⁵ x 14¹⁰

first floor

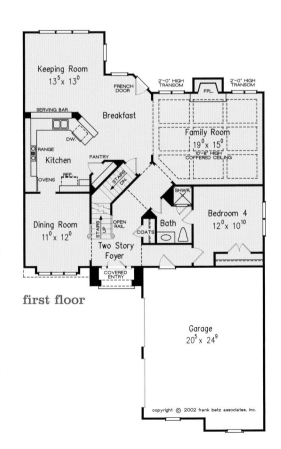

Keeping Room 13⁵ x 13⁰

Breakfast

Family Room 19⁰ x 15⁰ 10'-8" HIGH COFFERED CEILING

Kitchen

Dining Room 11⁰ x 12⁰

Two Story Foyer

Bath

Bedroom 4 12⁰ x 10¹⁰

Garage 20⁵ x 24⁹

copyright © 2002 frank betz associates, inc.

© Frank Betz Associates, Inc.

Sewell

Designer's Notes

Plan number: CAFB03-3732
PRICE CODE: **E**

Original and functional design details are what make the Sewell unique from its counterparts. The kitchen has the added upgrades that so many seek today, such as double ovens,

a built-in message center and decorative shelving. Three bedrooms share the upper level of the home, all with direct access to bathing areas and walk-in closets.

rear elevation

Bedrooms: 4

Baths: 3.5

Width: 50'-0"

Depth: 53'-0"

Main Level: 1838 sq ft

Second Level: 918 sq ft

Living Area: 2756 sq ft

first floor

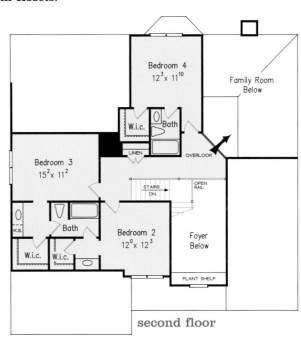

second floor

© Frank Betz Associates, Inc.

Windward

Designer's Notes

Plan number: CAFB03-3652
PRICE CODE: **F**

Cottage-style designs are defined by plans like the Windward. Fieldstone and cedar shake, accented by board-and-batten shutters, create the ideal cottage façade. The inside of this home is graced by many decorative columns that define its living spaces on the main floor. Optional bonus space is available on the upper level that can be finished into a playroom, exercise area or craft room.

rear elevation

Bedrooms: 4

Baths: 2.5

Width: 55'-0"

Depth: 54'-0"

Main Level: 1969 sq ft

Second Level: 894 sq ft

Living Area: 2863 sq ft

Opt. Bonus Room: 213 sq ft

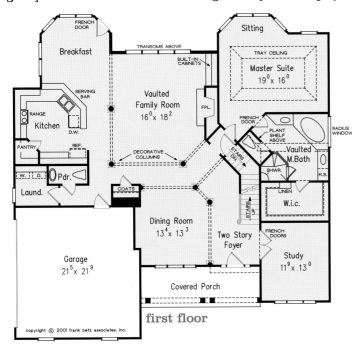

first floor

copyright © 2001 frank betz associates, inc.

second floor

Copeland

Designer's Notes

Plan number: CAFB03-3642
PRICE CODE: **E**

The clean and simple use of siding as the exterior or material combines well with the multi-angled roofline to create an inviting front elevation on the Copeland. A vaulted keeping room is nestled into the kitchen area, giving families a casual and comfortable spot to gather. A loft is incorporated upstairs that makes a great lounging area or homework station.

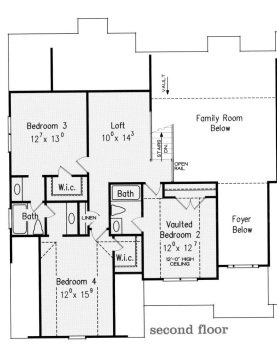

rear elevation

Bedrooms: 4

Baths: 3.5

Width: 62'-0"

Depth: 50'-4"

Main Level: 2024 sq ft

Second Level: 958 sq ft

Living Area: 2982 sq ft

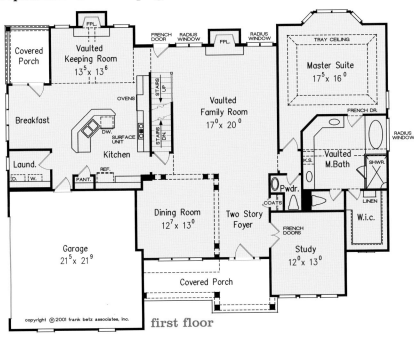

copyright © 2001 frank betz associates, inc.

first floor

second floor

© Frank Betz Associates, Inc.

Stone Bluff

Designer's Notes

Plan number: CAFB03-3658
PRICE CODE: **E**

Today's demanding lifestyles require a home that accommodates an active family. The Stone Bluff is thoughtfully designed with a large family room — canopied by a coffered ceiling

rear elevation

— that comfortably links to the kitchen and breakfast areas. The large kitchen — with an island and built-in message center — caters to today's busy family.

Bedrooms: 5

Baths: 4

Width: 60'-0"

Depth: 43'-10"

Main Level: 1448 sq ft

Second Level: 1714 sq ft

Living Area: 3162 sq ft

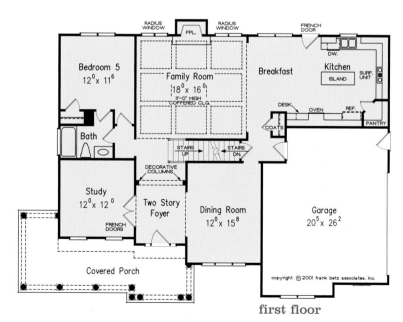
first floor

second floor

Seagraves

Designer's Notes

Plan number: CAFB03-3843
PRICE CODE: **F**

The Seagraves takes a step back in time with two stories of covered porches against red brick, giving it a colonial flair. A keeping room adjoins the kitchen, allowing families the perfect cozy place to gather and chat. A main-floor bedroom is a convenient location for a guest room. Telecommuters may opt to use this room as their home office.

rear elevation

Bedrooms: 5

Baths: 4.5

Width: 65'-6"

Depth: 59'-0"

Main Level: 1935 sq ft

Second Level: 1753 sq ft

Living Area: 3688 sq ft

first floor

second floor

Sweetwater (pages 60 to 61, 93) A cozy chenille - upholstered chair makes the perfect spot to curl up with a good book in the study.

Right | A covered front porch surrounded by stacked stone makes the ideal spot to watch children play in the front yard.

See page 76 for Sweetwater details.

Country

Country-style homes possess an unmistakable magnetism

that invites you to make yourself at home. Grand front porches, cheery dormers and classic materials suggest that all who enter should be prepared to kick up their feet – to be treated as family. Country façades are friendly, welcoming and reminiscent of times past.

But old-fashioned does not mean antiquated, for today's Country home is equipped with the family and guest-friendly amenities that our current market demands. Keeping rooms and children's retreats, mudrooms and master suites – today's Country home is ready for the entertainer and the growing family. It is adaptable to the needs of varied lifestyles, with plenty of flexible space that can be finished to the discretion of the homeowner. From curb appeal to craftsmanship, Country designs possess the look, feel and function of "*home.*"

McArthur Park

Designer's Notes

Plan number: CAFB03-3837
PRICE CODE: **D**

It has been said that beauty is often found in simplicity — and the McArthur Park brings truth to that statement. It's understated exterior and uncomplicated roofline make this home both appealing and cost - effective to build. The kitchen, breakfast area and keeping room share common space, making it ideal for entertaining. The dining room is defined by decorative columns, allowing effortless traffic flow. An optional bonus room is available on the upper floor that has endless possibilities. It can be easily finished as a fourth bedroom, playroom, exercise area or craft room.

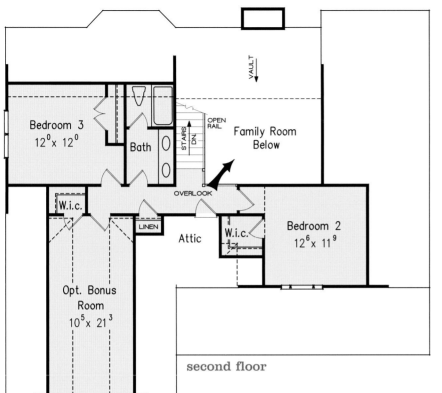

second floor

Bedroom 3
12⁰ x 12⁰

Bath

STAIRS DN

OPEN RAIL

VAULT

Family Room Below

OVERLOOK

W.i.c.

LINEN

Attic

W.i.c.

Bedroom 2
12⁶ x 11⁹

Opt. Bonus Room
10⁵ x 21³

rear elevation

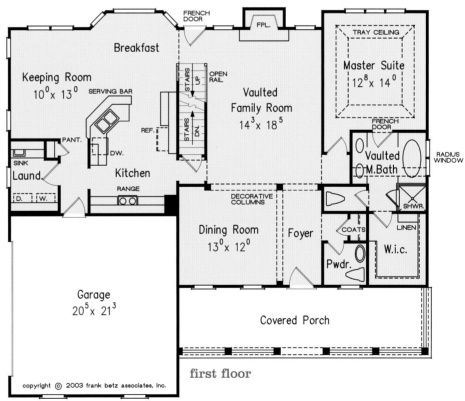

first floor

Breakfast

FRENCH DOOR

FPL.

TRAY CEILING

Keeping Room
10⁰ x 13⁰

SERVING BAR

STAIRS UP

OPEN RAIL

Master Suite
12⁸ x 14⁰

Vaulted Family Room
14³ x 18⁵

FRENCH DOOR

RADIUS WINDOW

PANT.

REF.

STAIRS DN

Vaulted M.Bath

SINK

DW.

Laund.

Kitchen

RANGE

SHWR.

LINEN

D. W.

DECORATIVE COLUMNS

COATS

Dining Room
13⁰ x 12⁰

Foyer

W.i.c.

Pwdr.

Garage
20⁵ x 21³

Covered Porch

copyright © 2003 frank betz associates, inc.

Bedrooms: 3

Baths: 2.5

Width: 52'-0"

Depth: 46'-4"

Main Level: 1480 sq ft

Second Level: 544 sq ft

Living Area: 2024 sq ft

Opt. Bonus Room: 253 sq ft

Defoors Mill

Designer's Notes

Plan number: CAFB03-3712
PRICE CODE: **E**

Tradition is appreciated in the thoughtful design of Defoors Mill. A covered porch is situated on the front of the home and leads to a charming and practical floor plan. The master suite encompasses an entire wing of the home for comfort and privacy. Its own private sitting area creates a quiet haven for homeowners to unwind after a busy day. An optional bonus room is available on the second floor, providing space to grow as the family does. Special details in this home include a handy island in the kitchen, decorative columns around the dining area and a coat closet just off the garage.

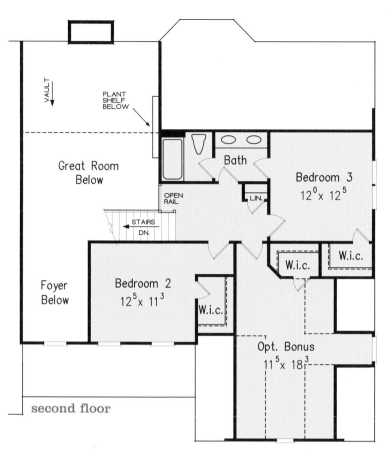

second floor

VAULT

Great Room Below

PLANT SHELF BELOW

Bath

Bedroom 3
12⁰ x 12⁵

LIN.

OPEN RAIL

STAIRS DN.

W.i.c.

W.i.c.

Foyer Below

Bedroom 2
12⁵ x 11³

W.i.c.

Opt. Bonus
11⁵ x 18³

rear elevation

RADIUS WINDOW

SEAT

SHWR.

Vaulted M.Bath

K.S.

His

PLANT SHELF ABOVE

Hers

LINEN

FPL

FRENCH DOOR

Breakfast

Bedroom 4/ Study
11⁶ x 11⁰

Vaulted Great Room
16⁰ x 19⁰

SERVING BAR

DW.

ISLAND

PANT.

RANGE

Kitchen

REF.

Bath

TRAY CEILING

Master Suite
13² x 15⁴

STAIRS UP

STAIRS DN.

COATS

Laund.

W.   D.

DECORATIVE COLUMNS

Two Story Foyer

Dining Room
12⁸ x 11³

Garage
20⁵ x 22³

Vaulted Sitting Area
13² x 10³

VAULT   VAULT

Covered Porch

first floor

copyright © 2002 frank betz associates, inc.

Bedrooms: 4

Baths: 3

Width: 55'-0"

Depth: 48'-0"

Main Level: 1803 sq ft

Second Level: 548 sq ft

Living Area: 2351 sq ft

Opt. Bonus Room: 277 sq ft

© Frank Betz Associates, Inc.

Bainbridge Court

Designer's Notes

Plan number: CAFB03-3815
PRICE CODE: **F**

From the Southern Living Design Collection™ – The classic brick-and-siding exterior of the Bainbridge Court gives this home a time-honored appeal. The staircase is strategically tucked away to keep the foyer open and roomy. A cozy screened porch adjoins the kitchen area and has access to an expansive deck, making a great space for grilling and entertaining. Two bedrooms — the master suite and a guest room — share the main level of the home. This guest room converts easily into a home office for the telecommuter, at-home mom or retiree. On the upper level, three well - placed bedrooms share a bath and enjoy overlook views into the family room.

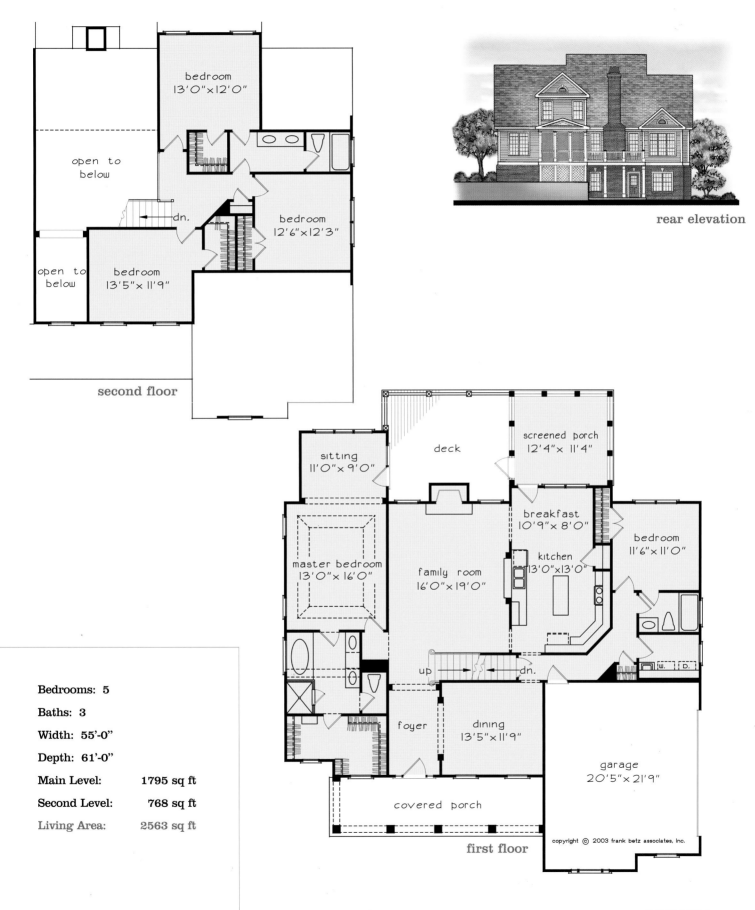

bedroom
13'0"×12'0"

open to below

dn.

open to below

bedroom
12'6"×12'3"

bedroom
13'5"×11'9"

second floor

rear elevation

sitting
11'0"×9'0"

deck

screened porch
12'4"×11'4"

breakfast
10'9"×8'0"

bedroom
11'6"×11'0"

master bedroom
13'0"×16'0"

family room
16'0"×19'0"

kitchen
13'0"×13'0"

up   **dn.**

foyer

dining
13'5"×11'9"

garage
20'5"×21'9"

covered porch

first floor

Bedrooms: 5

Baths: 3

Width: 55'-0"

Depth: 61'-0"

Main Level: 1795 sq ft

Second Level: 768 sq ft

Living Area: 2563 sq ft

Baldwin Farm

Designer's Notes

Plan number: CAFB03-3831
PRICE CODE: **G**

From the Southern Living Design Collection™ – Special accents borrowed from years gone by make the Baldwin Farm feel established and traditional. The carriage doors and cupola on the garage go back in time to give a historic elegance to the façade of this home. Some of today's most popular design trends are incorporated inside. The kitchen overlooks a cozy keeping room that adjoins a screened porch and deck — great for entertaining and relaxation. A mudroom is strategically situated inside the secondary entrance, keeping shoes and coats in their place. The second level of the home features a vaulted family entertainment room. Whether playing games, watching television or exercising, this is a spot where the whole family can enjoy their recreational time.

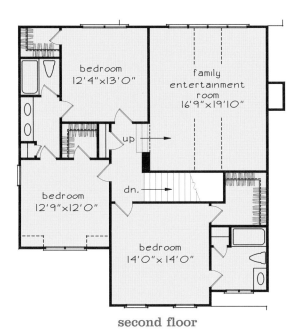

bedroom
12'4"×13'0"

family
entertainment
room
16'9"×19'10"

up

bedroom
12'9"×12'0"

dn.

bedroom
14'0"×14'0"

second floor

rear elevation

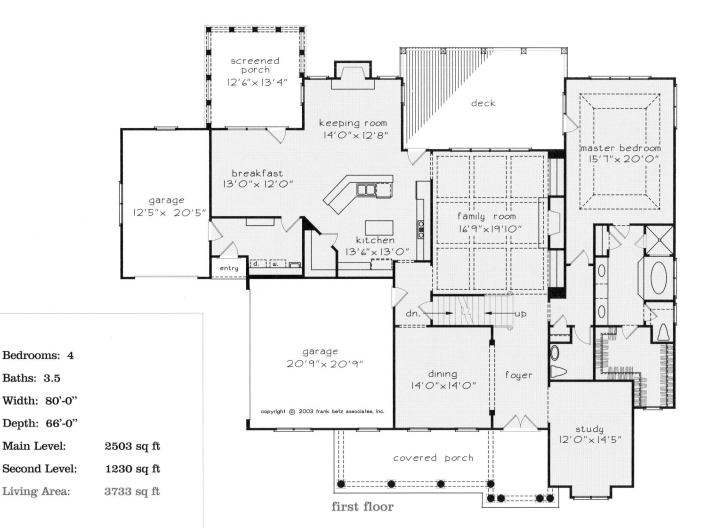

screened
porch
12'6"×13'4"

keeping room
14'0"×12'8"

deck

master bedroom
15'7"×20'0"

breakfast
13'0"×12'0"

garage
12'5"× 20'5"

kitchen
13'6"×13'0"

family room
16'9"×19'10"

entry

d. w.

dn.

up

garage
20'9"×20'9"

dining
14'0"×14'0"

foyer

study
12'0"×14'5"

copyright © 2003 frank betz associates, inc.

covered porch

first floor

Bedrooms: 4

Baths: 3.5

Width: 80'-0"

Depth: 66'-0"

Main Level: 2503 sq ft

Second Level: 1230 sq ft

Living Area: 3733 sq ft

© Frank Betz Associates, Inc.

rear elevation

Bedrooms: 3

Baths: 2.5

Width: 47'-0"

Depth: 34'-4"

Main Level: 729 sq ft

Second Level: 670 sq ft

Living Area: 1399 sq ft

Westwood

Designer's Notes

Plan number: CAFB03-1087
PRICE CODE: **A**

The Westwood's front porch and uncomplicated roof line make the exterior of this home welcoming and comfortable. Its formal dining room is just off the foyer, making an attractive and appealing first impression. A crackling fire in the great room is easily enjoyed from the breakfast area or kitchen.

second floor

first floor

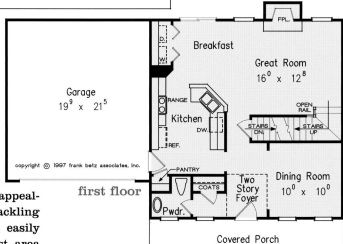

© Frank Betz Associates, Inc.

rear elevation

Bedrooms: 3

Baths: 2

Width: 52'-0"

Depth: 51'-0"

Main Level: 1540 sq ft

Living Area: 1540 sq ft

Riverglen

Designer's Notes

Plan number: CAFB03-3840
PRICE CODE: **B**

Fieldstone accents and dormers in the roofline give the Riverglen a feeling of home right from the start. High ceilings in the foyer, family room and dining room give this design a roomy feel from the minute you walk in. Access to the home from the garage is through the laundry room, keeping shoes and coats where they belong.

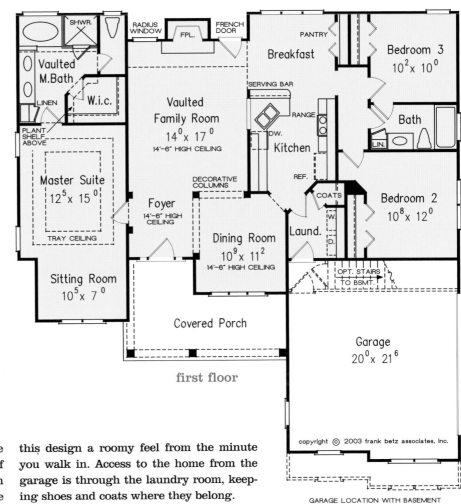

first floor

copyright © 2003 frank betz associates, inc.

GARAGE LOCATION WITH BASEMENT

© Frank Betz Associates, Inc.

rear elevation

Bedrooms: 3

Baths: 3

Width: 52'-4"

Depth: 49'-0"

Main Level: 1549 sq ft

Living Area: 1549 sq ft

Opt. Second Floor: 247 sq ft

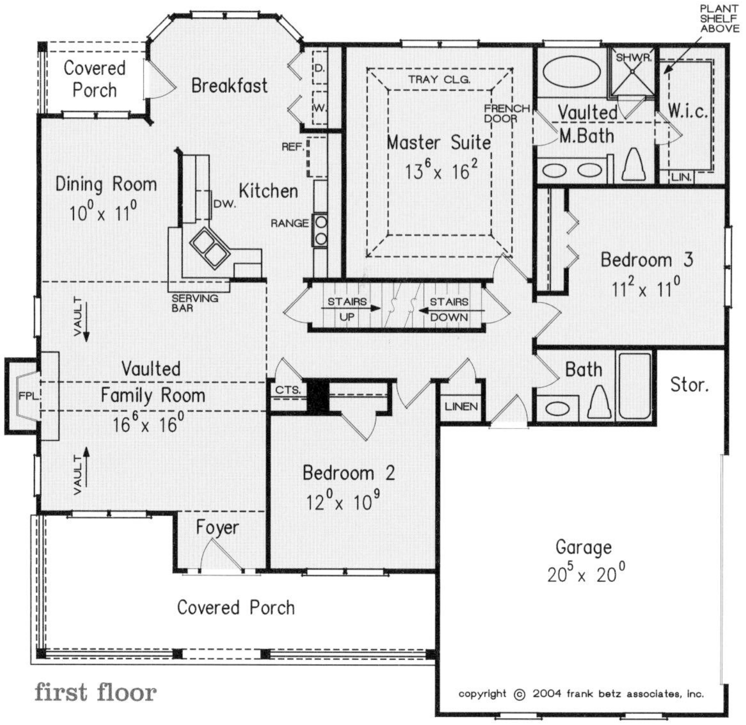

Overstreet

Designer's Notes

Plan number: CAFB03-3862

PRICE CODE: **B**

A wrap-around front porch and board-and-batten shutters are the defining details that make this home 100% country. A covered space on the rear of the home is accessed off the breakfast room and makes a great grilling porch. An optional second floor provides the possibility for a bonus room and an additional full bath.

first floor — floor plan labels:

Covered Porch · Breakfast · D. · DW. · TRAY CLG. · FRENCH DOOR · SHWR. · Vaulted M.Bath · W.i.c. · PLANT SHELF ABOVE · REF. · Master Suite 13⁶ x 16² · LIN. · Dining Room 10⁰ x 11⁰ · Kitchen · DW. · RANGE · Bedroom 3 11² x 11⁰ · SERVING BAR · STAIRS UP · STAIRS DOWN · Bath · Stor. · VAULT · FPL · Vaulted Family Room 16⁶ x 16⁰ · C.T.S. · LINEN · VAULT · Bedroom 2 12⁰ x 10⁹ · Foyer · Garage 20⁵ x 20⁰ · Covered Porch

copyright © 2004 frank betz associates, inc.

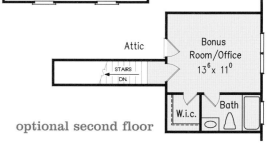

Attic · STAIRS DN. · Bonus Room/Office 13⁶ x 11⁰ · W.i.c. · Bath

optional second floor

© Frank Betz Associates, Inc.

rear elevation

Bedrooms: 4

Baths: 3

Width: 55'-0"

Depth: 55'-0"

Main Level: 1748 sq ft

Living Area: 1748 sq ft

Opt. Second Floor: 303 sq ft

Roswell

Designer's Notes

Plan number: CAFB03-3708

PRICE CODE: **C**

This charming split-bedroom design has traditional elements that are comforting and familiar. Holiday gatherings are easily accommodated in the formal dining room that is accented with a decorative column. The master suite has a bright and cheery window seat that makes the perfect spot to curl up with a good book.

first floor

optional second floor

© Frank Betz Associates, Inc.

rear elevation

Bedrooms: 3

Baths: 2

Width: 54'-0"

Depth: 56'-6"

Main Level: 1749 sq ft

Living Area: 1749 sq ft

Opt. Second Floor: 308 sq ft

Christal

DESIGNER'S NOTES

Plan number: CAFB03-1043
PRICE CODE: **C**

Charming dormers and a rocking-chair front porch make the Christal look like it could have been picked from the pages of yesteryear. An arched opening in the master suite leads to a secluded sitting area with a vaulted ceilings — a casual and quiet spot to relax. The laundry room buffers the garage from the rest of the home providing an appropriate spot to leave shoes and coats.

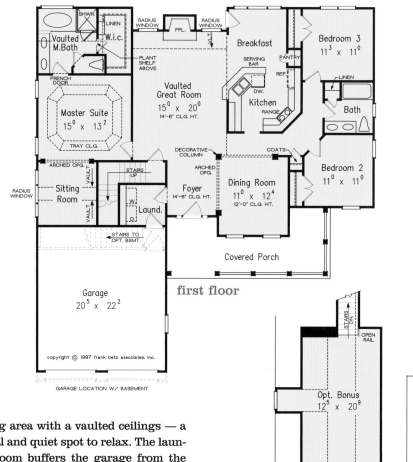

first floor

optional second floor

© Frank Betz Associates, Inc.

rear elevation

Bedrooms: 4

Baths: 3

Width: 50'-0"

Depth: 62'-6"

Main Level: 1792 sq ft

Living Area: 1792 sq ft

Opt. Second Floor: 255 sq ft

Powell

Designer's Notes

Plan number: CAFB03-3687
PRICE CODE: **B**

The Powell's charming dormers and cozy front porch provide a warm welcome to its residents and visitors. Thoughtful design details enhance the functionality of this home, including a handy coat closet in the foyer and the laundry room placed just off the garage. The optional bonus area makes an ideal guest suite or home office.

first floor

optional second floor

© Frank Betz Associates, Inc.

Sweetwater

Designer's Notes

Plan number: CAFB03-3691
PRICE CODE: **C**

Space, Sensibility, Style — that's what you'll find in the Sweetwater. The breakfast room opens to a large vaulted family room, giving growing families the space they need. Functional and practical amenities have been included, such as a kitchen island and built-in desk – that's sensibility. Special details such as decorative columns and art niches provide style!

rear elevation

Bedrooms: 4

Baths: 3

Width: 54'-4"

Depth: 36'-0"

Main Level: 1164 sq ft

Second Level: 916 sq ft

Living Area: 2080 sq ft

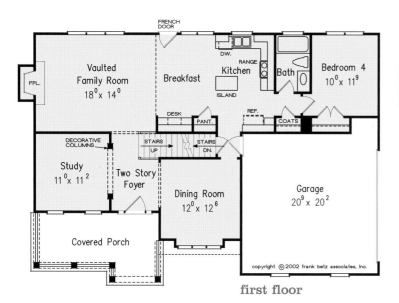

first floor

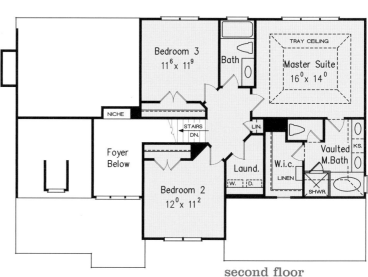

second floor

© Frank Betz Associates, Inc.

rear elevation

first floor

Bedrooms: 3

Baths: 2.5

Width: 63'-6"

Depth: 61'-0"

Main Level: 2170 sq ft

Living Area: 2170 sq ft

Designer's Notes
Plan number: CAFB03-1009
PRICE CODE: **E**

A rocking - chair front porch, coupled with traditional brick and dormers, is a friendly addition to any neighborhood. A bayed breakfast area is original and unique, with its tray ceiling and built-in message center to help keep the home-owner organized. Double ovens and an island in the kitchen offer more niceties.

© Frank Betz Associates, Inc.

rear elevation

first floor

Bedrooms: 4

Baths: 3.5

Width: 59'-4"

Depth: 73'-0"

Main Level: 2214 sq ft

Living Area: 2214 sq ft

Opt. Second Floor: 377 sq ft

Westvale

Designer's Notes

Plan number: CAFB03-3845
PRICE CODE: **D**

A classic blend of brick and siding, accented with dormers and a front porch, gives this home a traditional flair from the outside. Decorative columns surround the foyer and dining room creating a dramatic entrance. Casual family time is well spent in the keeping room situated just off the kitchen area.

optional second floor

© Frank Betz Associates, Inc.

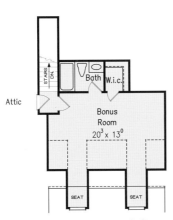

rear elevation

Bedrooms: 3

Baths: 3.5

Width: 59'-4"

Depth: 69'-0"

Main Level: 2275 sq ft

Living Area: 2275 sq ft

Opt. Second Floor: 407 sq ft

Walnut Grove

Designer's Notes

Plan number: CAFB03-3865
PRICE CODE: **D**

The Walnut Grove's cozy fieldstone exterior sets the stage for an equally impressive design inside. Two separate living spaces — the keeping and family rooms — give residents and guests alike options on where to gather. Double ovens and a serving bar in the kitchen make meal preparation and entertaining fun and easy.

optional second floor

Attic

Bath
W.i.c.
STAIRS DN.

Bonus
Room
20³ x 13⁰

SEAT   SEAT

first floor

FPL.

Keeping Room
13⁰ x 13⁶

TRAY CEILING

Master Suite
17⁰ x 14⁰

LINEN
TRAY CEILING

Breakfast

Covered Porch

FRENCH DOOR

QTR. RD. WINDOW

LINEN

FRENCH DOOR

W.i.c.

STAIRS UP
STAIRS DN

SERVING BAR
DW.

Kitchen
SURF. UNIT

Vaulted
Family Room
19³ x 15⁰

FPL

M.Bath

K.S.

OVENS
PANT.

REF.

QTR. RD. WINDOW

Pwdr.

W
D
Laund.
SHWR.
CTS.

DECORATIVE COLUMNS

Dining Room
13⁰ x 12⁴

Foyer

Bedroom 2
13⁰ x 11⁰

W.i.c.
LIN.

Bath

Garage
22⁸ x 21⁶

Covered Porch

Bedroom 3
13⁰ x 11⁰

copyright © 2004 frank betz associates, inc.

© Frank Betz Associates, Inc.

Dalrymple

Designer's Notes

Plan number: CAFB03-3833
PRICE CODE: **D**

Fieldstone and dormers accent the façade of the Dalrymple, giving it a warm and friendly charm. Adjoining the kitchen and breakfast room is a vaulted keeping room that provides an informal gathering spot for family and visitors. A sunken family room adds dimension and variety on the main floor, creating a higher ceiling and making the room feel spacious and roomy.

rear elevation

Bedrooms:	4
Baths:	3
Width:	54'-4"
Depth:	45'-6"
Main Level:	1353 sq ft
Second Level:	1072 sq ft
Living Area:	2425 sq ft
Opt. Bonus Room:	322 sq ft

copyright © 2003 frank betz associates, inc.

first floor

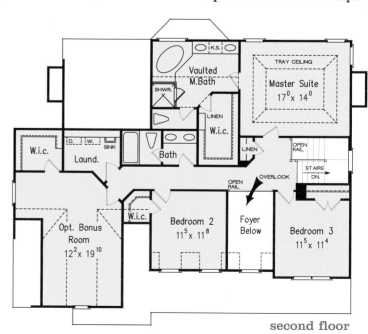

second floor

© Frank Betz Associates, Inc.

Germantown

Designer's Notes

Plan number: CAFB03-3726
PRICE CODE: **D**

The ageless façade of the Germantown has a certain congeniality to it that we are all familiar with, young and old. A vaulted keeping room with a fireplace is situated just off the kitchen, creating a friendly and casual place to gather with friends and family. The dining room is surrounded with decorative columns that gently define its borders.

rear elevation

Bedrooms: 4

Baths: 2.5

Width: 58'-4"

Depth: 49'-0"

Main Level: 1812 sq ft

Second Level: 779 sq ft

Living Area: 2591 sq ft

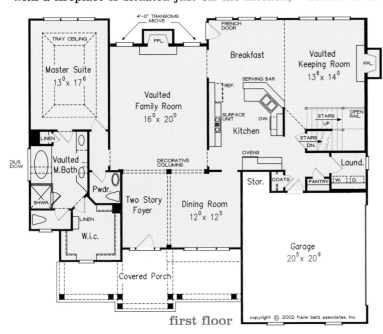

first floor

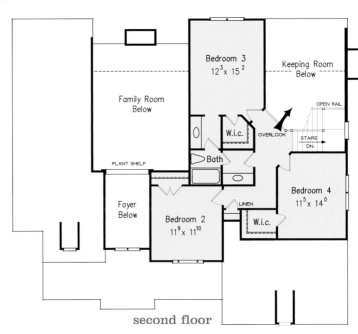

second floor

© Frank Betz Associates, Inc.

rear elevation

Bedrooms: 5

Baths: 4

Width: 54'-6"

Depth: 59'-4"

Main Level: 1409 sq ft

Second Level: 1300 sq ft

Living Area: 2709 sq ft

second floor

first floor

Kingston

Designer's Notes

Plan number: CAFB03-860
PRICE CODE: **D**

Few things say "country" more than a wrap-around porch! The Kingston's charming façade leads to a floor plan designed with common sense and practicality. A formal living just inside the entry can remain as such or be easily converted into a study. The fifth bedroom has access to a full bath, making it the perfect guest room.

© Frank Betz Associates, Inc.

Hyde Park

Designer's Notes

Plan number: CAFB03-3722
PRICE CODE: **E**

The Hyde Park's time-honored combination of siding and a wrap-around porch gives the feeling of a long-standing, established neighborhood that is once again so popular in today's newest communities. Inside, this design is roomy and open, with an overlook that is accessible from most rooms on the second level. Five bedrooms and four baths easily accommodate the growing family.

rear elevation

Bedrooms: 5

Baths: 4

Width: 58'-0"

Depth: 47'-6"

Main Level: 1393 sq ft

Second Level: 1332 sq ft

Living Area: 2725 sq ft

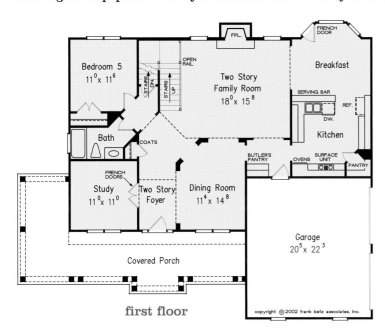

first floor

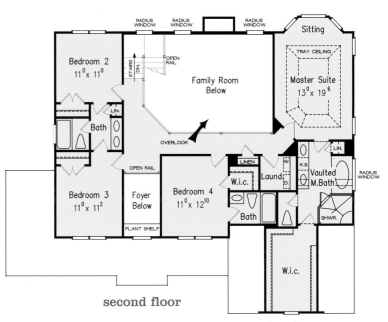

second floor

© Frank Betz Associates, Inc.

rear elevation

Bedrooms: 3

Baths: 3.5

Width: 68'-4"

Depth: 78'-0"

Main Level: 2745 sq ft

Living Area: 2745 sq ft

Opt. Second Floor: 374 sq ft

Allenbrook

Designer's Notes

Plan number: CAFB03-3849

PRICE CODE: **F**

Cheery dormers and a covered front porch give the Allenbrook a friendly, time-tested curb appeal. A fireplace lights the cozy keeping room that adjoins the kitchen area. The vaulted family room has an impressive wall of built-in cabinetry and another fireplace. Its split - bedroom design adds an aspect of privacy to the master suite.

optional second floor

first floor

© Frank Betz Associates, Inc.

rear elevation

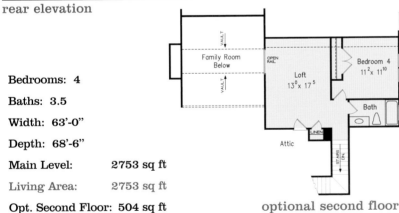

optional second floor

Bedrooms: 4

Baths: 3.5

Width: 63'-0"

Depth: 68'-6"

Main Level: 2753 sq ft

Living Area: 2753 sq ft

Opt. Second Floor: 504 sq ft

first floor

Wilson Bridge

Designer's Notes

Plan number: CAFB03-3846
PRICE CODE: **F**

The Wilson Bridge has many of the special details that make a house a home. Decorative columns are used to define the border between the foyer and dining room. A vaulted ceiling and fireplace make the keeping room a casual and cozy extension of the kitchen. Built-in cabinetry adds character to the family room, not to mention additional storage.

© Frank Betz Associates, Inc.

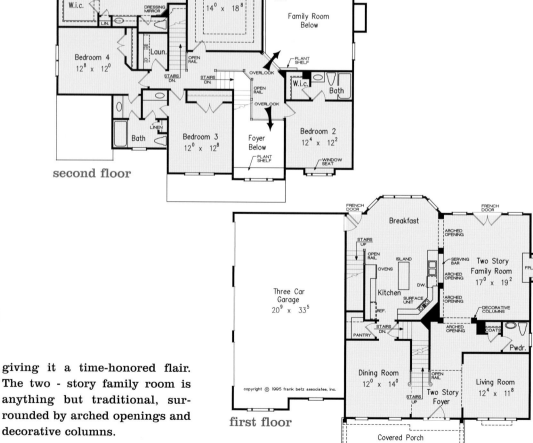

rear elevation

Bedrooms: 4

Baths: 3.5

Width: 58'-4"

Depth: 46'-6"

Main Level: 1347 sq ft

Second Level: 1493 sq ft

Living Area: 2840 sq ft

Opt. Bonus Room: 243 sq ft

Gentry

Designer's Notes

Plan number: CAFB03-913
PRICE CODE: **E**

A French - country warmth is often achieved by blending European stucco and stacked stone. Formal living and dining rooms border the two-story foyer giving it a time-honored flair. The two - story family room is anything but traditional, surrounded by arched openings and decorative columns.

second floor

first floor

copyright © 1995 frank betz associates, inc.

© Frank Betz Associates, Inc.

Ashton

Designer's Notes

Plan number: CAFB03-3598
PRICE CODE: **F**

Traditional on the outside and innovative on the inside, the Ashton incorporates the best of both worlds! A keeping room connects to the kitchen area, providing the per-fect place for relaxing family time. The master suite is truly luxurious with a bayed sitting area, his-and-her closets and a deco-rative art niche.

rear elevation

Bedrooms: 4

Baths: 3.5

Width: 61'-0"

Depth: 60'-4"

Main Level: 2146 sq ft

Second Level: 878 sq ft

Living Area: 3024 sq ft

Opt. Bonus Room: 341 sq ft

first floor

second floor

© Frank Betz Associates, Inc.

rear elevation

Bedrooms: 5

Baths: 4

Width: 65'-4"

Depth: 52'-0"

Main Level: 2140 sq ft

Second Level: 964 sq ft

Living Area: 3104 sq ft

Homestead

Designer's Notes

Plan number: CAFB03-3877

PRICE CODE: **E**

Its name says it all – this house has all the beauty, charisma and functionality that a homestead should have. A fireplace and radius window make the keeping room a cozy place to relax. The kitchen is fun for entertaining with its double ovens and serving bar. A multi-functional mudroom off the garage is complete with a coat closet, message center and bench.

first floor

second floor

© Frank Betz Associates, Inc.

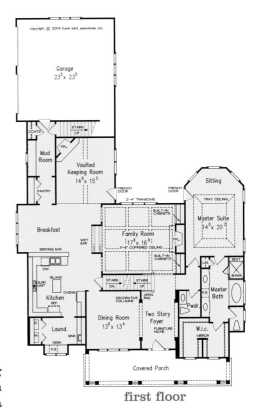

rear elevation

Bedrooms: 4

Baths: 3.5

Width: 55'-0"

Depth: 85'-0"

Main Level: 2284 sq ft

Second Level: 940 sq ft

Living Area: 3224 sq ft

Opt. Bonus Room: 545 sq ft

Crawford Heights

Designer's Notes

Plan number: CAFB03-3858
PRICE CODE: **E**

Style and function come together in the Crawford Heights to create a home that is as practical as it is beautiful. Coffered ceilings, a wet bar and built-in cabinetry make the family room an ideal gathering spot. The laundry room has a built-in sink and message center, making this a multi-purpose area.

second floor

first floor

© Frank Betz Associates, Inc.

Berkleigh Hills

Designer's Notes

Plan number: CAFB03-3870
PRICE CODE: **E**

Three cheery dormers and a covered front porch give the Berkleigh Hills that friendly curb appeal that a home should have. A vaulted keeping room – with a fireplace and transom windows – borders the kitchen area, giving family and guests a casual and comfortable place to gather. A coffered ceiling in the family room adds dimension and character to the room.

rear elevation

Bedrooms: 4

Baths: 3.5

Width: 65'-0"

Depth: 56'-10"

Main Level: 2298 sq ft

Second Level: 1039 sq ft

Living Area: 3337 sq ft

first floor

second floor

© Frank Betz Associates, Inc.

rear elevation

Bedrooms: 4

Baths: 4.5

Width: 70'-0"

Depth: 82'-0"

Main Level: 2521 sq ft

Second Level: 1116 sq ft

Living Area: 3637 sq ft

Opt. Bonus Room: 650 sq ft

second floor

first floor

Northfield

Designer's Notes

Plan number: CAFB03-3855
PRICE CODE: **F**

Attention entertainers! This might just be the home for you. An open and unobstructed arrangement of rooms on the main floor makes this an ideal home for entertaining. The large kitchen overlooks a uniquely shaped breakfast area, as well as a vaulted keeping room. This entire space flows easily into the family room, with a coffered ceiling that makes a dramatic statement.

© Frank Betz Associates, Inc.

Brookshire Manor

Designer's Notes

Plan number: CAFB03-1184
PRICE CODE: **G**

Class, style, tradition and every creature comfort imaginable – the Brookshire Manor grants every wish! Relax and unwind by the fire in the cozy hearth room adjoining the kitchen. The master suite earns its name featuring a personal lounging room with a fireplace, a lavish master bath with private dressing area, and direct access to the exercise room. A covered wrap-around porch and its gambrel roof over the garage make the façade welcoming.

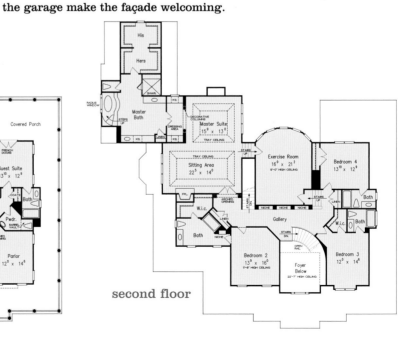

rear elevation

Bedrooms: 5

Baths: 5.5

Width: 85'-0"

Depth: 85'-6"

Main Level: 2732 sq ft

Second Level: 2734 sq ft

Living Area: 5466 sq ft

first floor

second floor

Sweetwater (pages 60 to 61, 93) Cedar shakes, stacked stone and board-and-batten shutters unite to form a down-to-earth, wholesome front elevation.

Top | Warm wood tones throughout the kitchen coupled with clean-lined window treatments create an uncomplicated and comfortable gathering place.

Above | Olive - hued cabinetry serves as an eye-catching focal point of the family room.

See page 76 for Sweetwater details.

Gastonia (pages 94 to 95, 115) An equestrian themed room uses an appealing combination of red, gold and black to generate a unique space for guests to enjoy.

Visit www.homeswithcurbappeal.com for complete details on the Gastonia.

Right | Carmel Battered columns atop sturdy stone pillars surround a front porch that is fully equipped for rocking chairs and long conversation.

Craftsman

The uncomplicated rooflines and robust front porches of

the Craftsman-style home takes us back to a place in history where society longed for an escape from its more formal predecessor, the Victorian. Sturdy porch columns replaced pristine spindles, and functional, mission-style windows took the place of ornamental ones. The home became as simplified as the lifestyles were. Popularized by architect Gustav Stickley in the early 1900s, he writes that the Craftsman home represents, "...a house reduced to its simplest form...its low, broad proportions and absolute lack of ornamentation gives it a character so natural and unaffected that it seems to...blend with any landscape."

The Craftsman style has regained its popularity in the 21st Century as we, once again, seek to simplify our living spaces. The wholesomeness of the façade and minimalist design bring a refreshing release to harried lifestyles.

Palmdale

Designer's Notes

Plan number: CAFB03-3776
PRICE CODE: **C**

Special details and added extras give the Palmdale an edge over its one-level competitors. It's exterior blend of cedar shake, siding and brick come together to create a warm and welcoming façade. Step inside to find exceptional floor planning and details. A unique niche is incorporated into the foyer, providing the ideal location for that special furniture piece or artwork. Transom windows allow extra light to pour into the family room. A generously sized optional bonus area provides an additional bedroom, a home office or exercise room.

Opt.
Bedroom 4
13^3 x 15^0

STAIRS DN.

OPEN RAIL

Opt.
Bath

Opt.
W.i.c.

Attic

optional second floor

rear elevation

TRAY CEILING

2'-0" TRANSOMS ABOVE

FRENCH DOOR

FPL.

FRENCH DOOR

W.i.c.

PANT.

Breakfast

Bedroom 3
13^3 x 11^3

Master Suite
14^5 x 17^0

SERVING BAR

LINEN

Bath

FRENCH DOOR

SEAT

Family Room
15^0 x 19^8
13'-2" HIGH CEILING

DW.

Kitchen

RANGE

LINEN

SHWR.

REF.

STAIRS UP

Bedroom 2
13^3 x 12^0

RADIUS TRANSOM ABOVE

Vaulted
M.Bath

Pwdr.

Foyer
13'-2" HIGH CEILING

Dining Room
12^9 x 12^0

STAIRS DN.

COATS

Laund.

W. D.

W.i.c.

W.i.c.

FURNITURE NICHE

Covered Porch

first floor

Garage
20^5 x 21^3

copyright © 2003 frank betz associates, inc.

Bedrooms: 4

Baths: 3.5

Width: 59'-0"

Depth: 57'-0"

Main Level: 2073 sq ft

Living Area: 2073 sq ft

Opt. Second Floor: 350 sq ft

© Frank Betz Associates, Inc.

Pasadena

Designer's Notes

Plan number: CAFB03-3756
PRICE CODE: **E**

Charm and character abound from the façade of the Pasadena with its tapered architectural columns and carriage doors. Inside, the master suite is tucked away on the rear of the main level, giving the homeowner a peaceful place to unwind. An art niche is situated in the breakfast area, providing the perfect spot for a favorite art piece or floral arrangement. The kitchen is complete with a large island, making mealtime easier. Upstairs, an optional bonus room has been made available that can be used as the homeowner wishes – a playroom, home office or fitness room are all fantastic options.

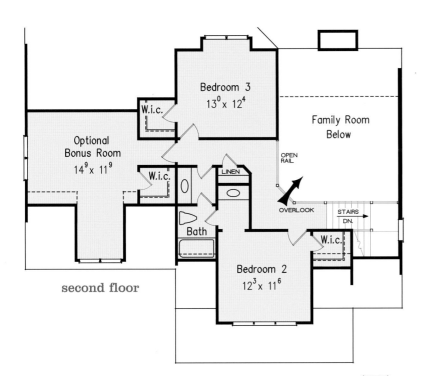

second floor

Bedroom 3
13^0 x 12^4

W.i.c.

Optional Bonus Room
14^9 x 11^9

W.i.c.

LINEN

Family Room Below

OPEN RAIL

OVERLOOK

STAIRS DN.

Bath

W.i.c.

Bedroom 2
12^3 x 11^6

rear elevation

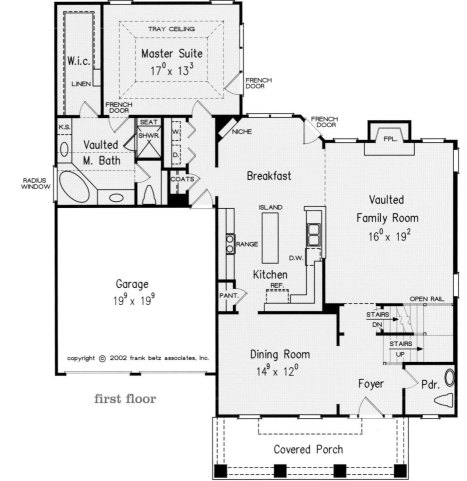

W.i.c.

LINEN

TRAY CEILING

Master Suite
17^0 x 13^3

FRENCH DOOR

FRENCH DOOR

K.S.

Vaulted M. Bath

SEAT

SHWR.

W.

D.

COATS

RADIUS WINDOW

NICHE

FRENCH DOOR

FPL.

Breakfast

Vaulted Family Room
16^0 x 19^2

ISLAND

RANGE

D.W.

Kitchen

REF.

PANT.

Garage
19^9 x 19^9

copyright © 2002 frank betz associates, inc.

first floor

OPEN RAIL

STAIRS DN

STAIRS UP

Dining Room
14^9 x 12^0

Foyer

Pdr.

Covered Porch

Bedrooms: 3

Baths: 2.5

Width: 50'-0"

Depth: 57'-0"

Main Level: 1561 sq ft

Second Level: 578 sq ft

Living Area: 2139 sq ft

Opt. Bonus Room: 274 sq ft

© Frank Betz Associates, Inc.

Bakersfield

Designer's Notes

Plan number: CAFB03-3783
PRICE CODE: **D**

The Craftsman style - home has made a comeback! Tapered columns and prairie - type windows, combined with earthen stone and cedar shakes, make the Bakersfield reminiscent of the craftsman era. A two-story foyer with an art niche creates an exciting first impression. Relaxing family time is well spent in the keeping room – which is strategically placed just off the kitchen for easy interaction from room to room. A bedroom connected to a full bath is incorporated into the main floor, making an ideal guest suite. How "suite" it is to relax in the master bedroom! Tray ceilings and a private lounging area make this a true retreat.

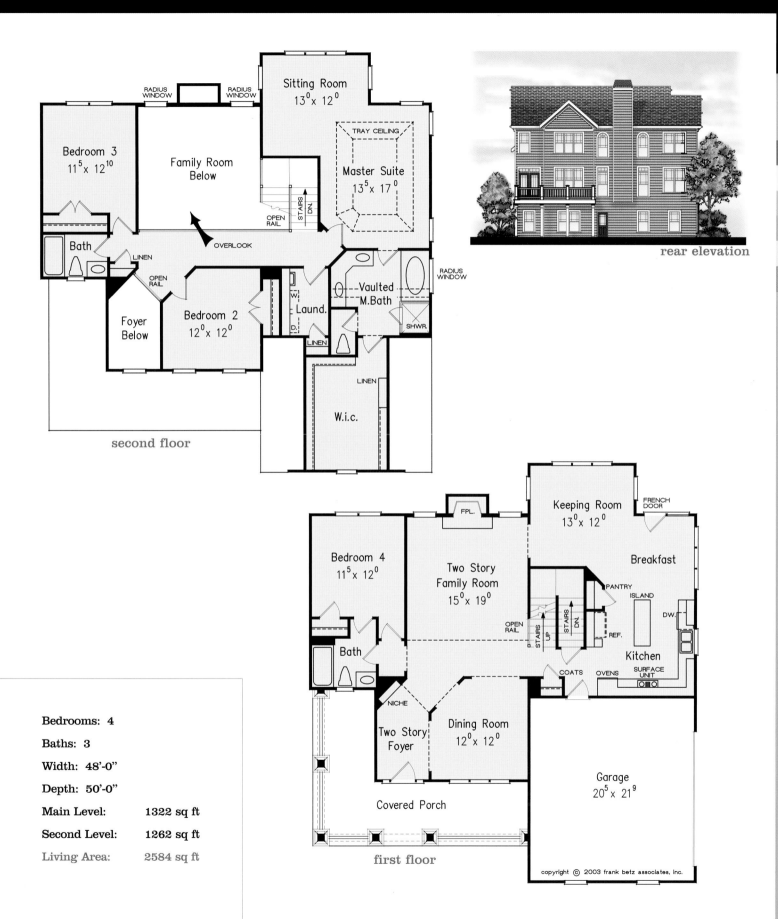

Bedroom 3
11^5 x 12^{10}

RADIUS WINDOW

RADIUS WINDOW

Sitting Room
13^0 x 12^0

Family Room Below

TRAY CEILING

Master Suite
13^5 x 17^0

OPEN RAIL

STAIRS DN.

Bath

LINEN

OVERLOOK

OPEN RAIL

Foyer Below

Bedroom 2
12^0 x 12^0

W.

D.

Laund.

Vaulted M.Bath

RADIUS WINDOW

SHWR.

LINEN

LINEN

W.i.c.

second floor

rear elevation

FPL.

Keeping Room
13^0 x 12^0

FRENCH DOOR

Bedroom 4
11^5 x 12^0

Two Story Family Room
15^0 x 19^0

Breakfast

PANTRY

ISLAND

DW.

Bath

OPEN RAIL

STAIRS UP

STAIRS DN.

REF.

Kitchen

COATS

OVENS

SURFACE UNIT

NICHE

Two Story Foyer

Dining Room
12^0 x 12^0

Garage
20^5 x 21^9

Covered Porch

first floor

copyright © 2003 frank betz associates, inc.

Bedrooms: 4

Baths: 3

Width: 48'-0"

Depth: 50'-0"

Main Level: 1322 sq ft

Second Level: 1262 sq ft

Living Area: 2584 sq ft

Braxtons Creek

Designer's Notes

Plan number: CAFB03-3851
PRICE CODE: **E**

From the Southern Living Design Collection™ – The attractive combination of cedar shake and stone with prairie - style accents gives the Braxtons Creek the Craftsman appeal that is in high demand today. Tapered architectural columns and unique, prairie - style windows give this home an original look. A vaulted keeping room is arranged just off the kitchen and breakfast areas of the home. With a fireplace and serene views to the backyard, this is a warm and comfortable family gathering spot. Upstairs, an optional bedroom and bath make the perfect guest suite or can be easily converted into a home office. A children's retreat can be added as well, giving kids the perfect place to enjoy games, videos or computer fun.

bedroom
13'4"x13'3"

children's retreat
18'6"x14'2"

dn.

attic

optional second floor

rear elevation

deck

breakfast
13'4"x12'0"

keeping room
14'0"x13'10"

master bedroom
13'8" 17'0"

family room
15'9"x18'5"

up

kitchen
13'4"x14'3"

dn.

bedroom
14'0"x12'0"

foyer

dining
12'3"x13'0"

bedroom
15'3"x11'6"

covered porch

first floor

garage
21'5"x 27'3"

copyright © 2003 frank betz associates, inc.

Bedrooms: 4

Baths: 3.5

Width: 66'-4"

Depth: 83'-0"

Main Level: 2660 sq ft

Living Area: 2660 sq ft

Opt. Second Floor: 610 sq ft

© Frank Betz Associates, Inc.

rear elevation

Bedrooms: 3

Baths: 2

Width: 48'-0"

Depth: 35'-4"

Main Level: 1273 sq ft

Lower Level: 47 sq ft

Living Area: 1320 sq ft

Sherman Oaks

Designer's Notes

Plan number: CAFB03-3826
PRICE CODE: **B**

Tapered architectural columns, eave brackets and cedar shake give this split-foyer design a fresh and innovative appeal. Corner windows over the sink provide great views to the backyard. Sliding glass doors off the dining room and kitchen area make outdoor dining fun and accessible.

first floor

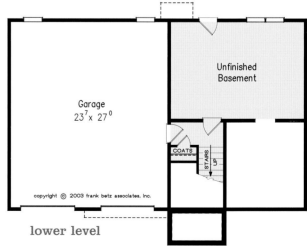

lower level

© Frank Betz Associates, Inc.

rear elevation

Bedrooms: 3

Baths: 2

Width: 53'-6"

Depth: 58'-6"

Main Level: 1724 sq ft

Living Area: 1724 sq ft

Opt. Bonus Room: 375 sq ft

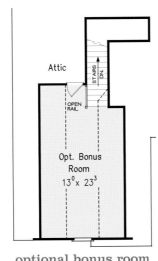

optional bonus room

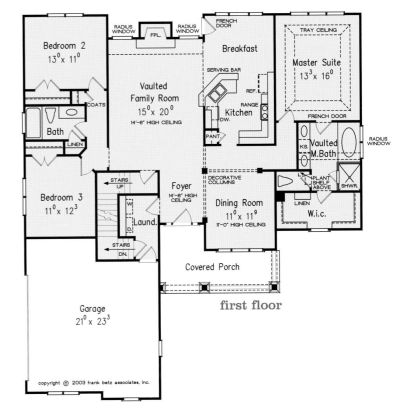

first floor

Oxnard

Designer's Notes

Plan number: CAFB03-3819
PRICE CODE: **B**

One look at the Oxnard and you'll see the difference between a house and a home. A split-bedroom design, the master suite encompasses one side of the home, while the additional bedrooms share the other. Common living space is situated between them. Decorative columns subtly separate the dining room from its neighboring foyer.

© Frank Betz Associates, Inc.

rear elevation

Bedrooms: 4

Baths: 3

Width: 56'-10"

Depth: 45'-6"

Main Level: 1404 sq ft

Second Level: 959 sq ft

Living Area: 2363 sq ft

Opt. Bonus Room: 374 sq ft

Modesto

Designer's Notes

Plan number: CAFB03-3803
PRICE CODE: **D**

This home is well-planned in its design with liberal room dimensions throughout its two stories. A highlight in the kitchen is the large prep island, taking some of the stress out of meals and entertaining. An optional bonus room upstairs gives homeowners some flexible space to finish as they wish.

second floor

LINEN
SHWR.
Vaulted M.Bath
W.i.c.
PLANT SHELF ABOVE
LINEN
KS.
FRENCH DOOR
W.i.c.
Bedroom 3
12⁰ x 11⁵
Bath
OVER-LOOK
STAIRS DN.
OPEN RAIL
W.i.c.
Opt. Bonus Room
19⁹ x 15⁵
Master Suite
13⁰ x 17⁰
TRAY CEILING
Foyer Below
Bedroom 2
13⁰ x 11⁹
SEAT

first floor

FRENCH DOOR
Breakfast
Bath
Bedroom 4/ Study
11⁴ x 12⁰
Family Room
20⁵ x 15⁰
ISLAND
DW.
COATS
FPL.
SERVING BAR
Kitchen
RANGE
REF.
PANTRY
STAIRS DN.
W.
D.
Living Room
13⁰ x 11⁹
STAIRS UP
BUTLER'S PANTRY
Garage
19⁹ x 21⁹
Two Story Foyer
Dining Room
13⁰ x 11⁹
copyright © 2003 frank betz associates, inc.
Covered Porch

© Frank Betz Associates, Inc.

rear elevation

Bedrooms: 4

Baths: 3.5

Width: 62'-6"

Depth: 77'-4"

Main Level: 2395 sq ft

Living Area: 2395 sq ft

Opt. Second Floor: 660 sq ft

Camden Lake

Designer's Notes

Plan number: CAFB03-3828

PRICE CODE: **E**

Beamed gables and cedar shake create an appealing Craftsman - style elevation on the Camden Lake. Double ovens, a serving bar and a liberally sized pantry make the kitchen a user-friendly room. Its view to the cozy keeping room warms the entire space, creating an inviting environment.

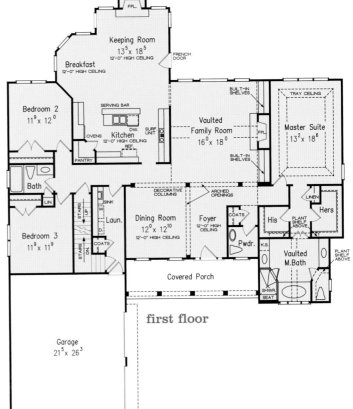

optional second floor

first floor

© Frank Betz Associates, Inc.

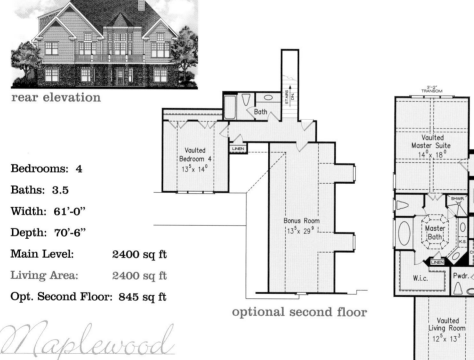

rear elevation

Bedrooms: 4

Baths: 3.5

Width: 61'-0"

Depth: 70'-6"

Main Level: 2400 sq ft

Living Area: 2400 sq ft

Opt. Second Floor: 845 sq ft

Maplewood

Designer's Notes

Plan number: CAFB03-3878

PRICE CODE: **D**

The Maplewood's inviting exterior is just a taste of what's waiting inside. Transom windows along the back of the home welcome in plenty of sun-shine, brightening each room. A cof-fered ceiling, fireplace and built-in cabinetry in the family room make for an attractive center point of the home.

optional second floor

- Bath
- STAIRS DN
- LINEN
- Vaulted Bedroom 4 13⁵ x 14⁰
- Bonus Room 13⁵ x 29⁹

first floor

- 3'-2" TRANSOM
- W.i.c.
- LINEN
- Bedroom 2 12⁰ x 11¹⁰
- Vaulted Master Suite 14⁰ x 18⁰
- 3'-2" TRANSOMS
- 3'-2" TRANSOM
- FRENCH DOOR
- Vaulted Breakfast
- Bath
- SERVING BAR
- SHWR.
- FPL.
- Family Room 16⁰ x 19⁴ 14'-5" HIGH COFFERED CEILING
- BUILT-IN CABINETS
- REF.
- DW.
- SURF. UNIT
- STAIRS UP
- STAIRS DN
- Bedroom 3 12⁰ x 12¹⁰
- Master Bath
- K.S.
- Kitchen
- PANTRY
- W.i.c.
- LINEN
- COATS
- OVENS
- fw. td. SINK
- Laund.
- Pwdr.
- DECORATIVE COLUMNS
- Foyer
- Dining Room 14⁸ x 12⁰
- FURNITURE NICHE
- Vaulted Living Room 12⁵ x 13³
- Covered Porch
- Garage 22⁵ x 29⁸

copyright © 2004 frank betz associates, inc.

TO ORDER PLANS CALL TOLL FREE 888-717-3003

© Frank Betz Associates, Inc.

Carmel

Designer's Notes

Plan number: CAFB03-3847
PRICE CODE: **D**

Tapered columns and triple dormers are the eye-catching exterior highlights of the Carmel. A generous kitchen area accommodates families of all sizes with its double ovens, cook - top island and vaulted breakfast area. A computer loft and bookshelves have been incorporated into the upper level of the home, making the ideal home-work station for children.

rear elevation

Bedrooms: 3

Baths: 2.5

Width: 56'-0"

Depth: 56'-6"

Main Level: 1862 sq ft

Second Level: 661 sq ft

Living Area: 2523 sq ft

Opt. Bonus Room: 315 sq ft

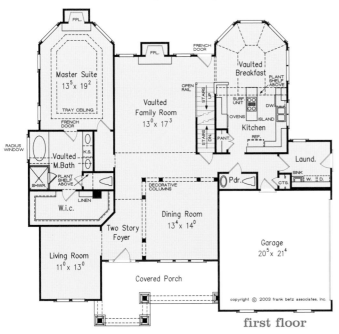

first floor

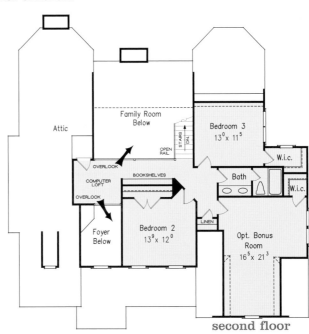

second floor

© Frank Betz Associates, Inc.

rear elevation

Bedrooms: 4

Baths: 3

Width: 55'-4"

Depth: 55'-0"

Main Level: 1464 sq ft

Second Level: 1164 sq ft

Living Area: 2628 sq ft

Mulholland

Designer's Notes

Plan number: CAFB03-3838

PRICE CODE: **D**

The Mulholland is a design that was generated with today's family in mind. Watch the kids play from your rocking - chair front porch surrounded by tapered architectural columns. A bedroom on the main floor makes an ideal location for a home office or guest room with its adjoining full bath.

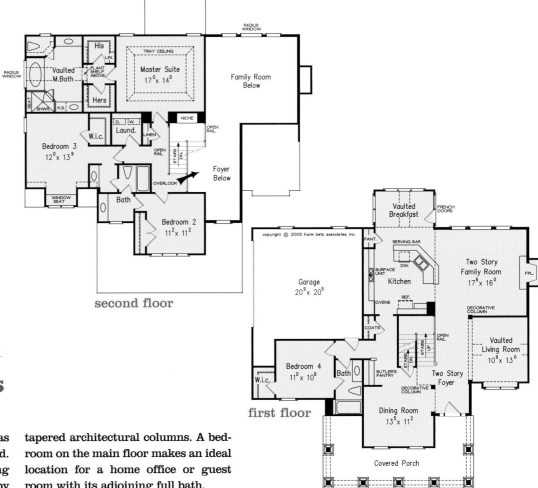

second floor

first floor

© Frank Betz Associates, Inc.

Del Ray

Designer's Notes

Plan number: CAFB03-3830
PRICE CODE: **D**

The Del Ray defines the look of a Craftsman - style home with its tapered columns and timber - accented gables. A main - floor bedroom is the ideal location for a guest room with its neighboring full bath. The simple addition of French doors in the living room makes an easy conversion into a study. A large laundry room is incorporated in the upper level, centrally located among the bedrooms.

rear elevation

Bedrooms: 5

Baths: 3

Width: 49'-0"

Depth: 49'-0"

Main Level: 1405 sq ft

Second Level: 1226 sq ft

Living Area: 2631 sq ft

first floor

second floor

© Frank Betz Associates, Inc.

rear elevation

Bedrooms: 4

Baths: 2.5

Width: 57'-4"

Depth: 39'-0"

Main Level: 1249 sq ft

Second Level: 1458 sq ft

Living Area: 2707 sq ft

Sonoma

Designer's Notes

Plan number: CAFB03-3798
PRICE CODE: **E**

The Sonoma is an eye-catcher because of its well-balanced, clean-lined exterior. Arched openings separate the family room from the kitchen area, where you'll find double ovens, an island and built-in message center. A vaulted sitting area AND a covered porch adjoin the master suite, making this space live up to its name!

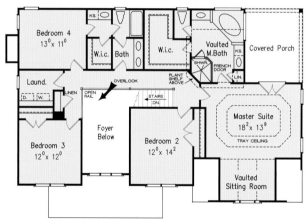

second floor

first floor

© Frank Betz Associates, Inc.

rear elevation

Bedrooms: 4

Baths: 3.5

Width: 46'-4"

Depth: 66'-0"

Main Level: 1243 sq ft

Second Level: 1474 sq ft

Living Area: 2717 sq ft

Ventura

Designer's Notes

Plan number: CAFB03-3799

PRICE CODE: **E**

Unique details are what distinguish this home from its other two - story counterparts. A barrel - vaulted ceiling canopies the hallway leading from the foyer to the family room. A separate entrance, located on the side of the Ventura, enters through the laundry room — perfect for the daily comings and goings of family members.

second floor

first floor

© Frank Betz Associates, Inc.

rear elevation

Bedrooms: 4

Baths: 2.5

Width: 58'-0"

Depth: 45'-6"

Main Level: 1367 sq ft

Second Level: 1492 sq ft

Living Area: 2859 sq ft

second floor

Santa Clara

Designer's Notes

Plan number: CAFB03-3841
PRICE CODE: **E**

Eave brackets enhance the gabled roofline – a time - honored design technique that has made a welcomed comeback. The kitchen area is easily accessed from both the family room and the breakfast area, creating one common space for families to share their time. The laundry room, a powder room and a coat closet are thoughtfully situated just off the garage.

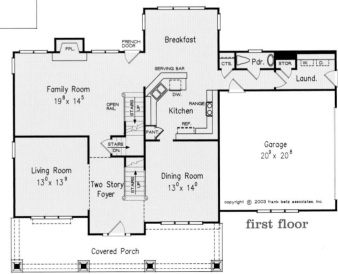

first floor

Gastonia (pages 94 to 95, 115) Built-in cabinetry and a writing desk make this study functional while maintaining its simplicity.

Top | Casual yet elegant floral fabrics make this formal living room a not-too-formal gathering place to visit with friends and family.

Above | A round table surrounded by upholstered chairs makes entertaining fun and interactive in the dining room.

Elam Cool tones of gray and green pair up in the two-story family room making a more formal spot to entertain guests.

Right | Black shutters against creamy white stucco make a bold and dignified statement to pedestrians.

Visit www.homeswithcurbappeal.com for complete details on the Elam.

Old World

The influence of European architecture is what defines

the personality and character of an Old World design. Castle-like turrets are encased by stately stonework or classic European stucco. Visions of vintage French architecture come to mind when earthy tones or sturdy brick are accented with quoins or covered entries. An Old World design presents a slightly more formal approach from the curb, without being pretentious or stuffy. Creative combinations of varied exterior materials generate historic warmth and charisma.

Modern features accompany these time-honored façades to create homes that are livable and practical. Volume ceilings, cozy hearth rooms, centralized message centers and family recreation rooms make these Old World designs new again. Screened porches, Jack-and-Jill baths and gourmet kitchens launch these vintage-looking homes straight into the 21st Century. Design details combine with age-old façades to create functional, family-friendly homes that are high on the wish list of today's homeowner.

© Frank Betz Associates, Inc.

Barnsworth

Designer's Notes

Plan number: CAFB03-3850
PRICE CODE: **C**

The Old World style is communicated by using accents borrowed from yesteryear to create an established look. Fieldstone and louvered shutters are the perfect features to create that Old World charm on the Barnsworth. Decorative columns border the entry to the dining room, making an impressive first impression. A vaulted keeping room just off the kitchen area gives family and friends a comfortable spot to congregate after dinner. An optional bonus area is available over the garage that can be used to your discretion. A home office, exercise room or play room would all be easily accommodated by this space.

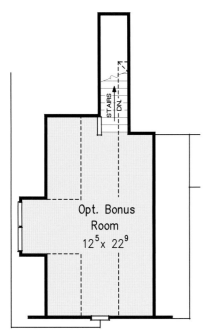

Opt. Bonus
Room
12^5 x 22^9

STAIRS DN.

optional second floor

rear elevation

Bedrooms: 3

Baths: 2

Width: 54'-6"

Depth: 60'-0"

Main Level: 2034 sq ft

Living Area: 2034 sq ft

Opt. Second Floor: 310 sq ft

RADIUS WINDOW

TRAY CEILING

Master Suite
13^6 x 16^0

FRENCH DOOR

Breakfast

FPL.

Vaulted
Great Room
15^0 x 19^{10}
15'-0" HIGH CEILING

Vaulted
Keeping Room
13^8 x 16^0

SERVING BAR

RANGE

Kitchen

DW.

RADIUS WINDOW

Vaulted
M.Bath

SHWR.

PLANT SHELF ABOVE

LINEN

W.i.c.

FRENCH DOOR

STAIRS UP

W
D.

Laund.

COATS

STAIRS DN.

Vaulted
Foyer
15'-0" HIGH CEILING

PANT.

REF.

STOR.

Bedroom 3
11^5 x 11^0

DECORATIVE COLUMNS

Dining Room
11^0 x 11^6

Bath

LIN.

Bedroom 2
11^5 x 11^6

Covered Porch

Garage
20^5 x 20^9

first floor

copyright © 2003 frank betz associates, inc.

© Frank Betz Associates, Inc.

Catawba Ridge

Designer's Notes

Plan number: CAFB03-3823
PRICE CODE: **F**

From the Southern Living Design Collection™ – Charm and character exude from the inviting exterior of Catawba Ridge with its welcoming combination of stone and cedar shake. A cozy front porch graces the front of the home. Inside, the kitchen, breakfast area and family room are conveniently grouped together for easy family interaction. Just off the breakfast area is a comfy screened porch – the perfect spot to end a busy day. The master suite encompasses one entire wing of the home, giving the homeowner added privacy. Kids will love having their own designated spot to do homework in the computer loft upstairs. An optional bonus room is ready to finish on the upper level, ideal for a fourth bedroom, play area or exercise room.

TO ORDER PLANS CALL TOLL FREE 888-717-3003

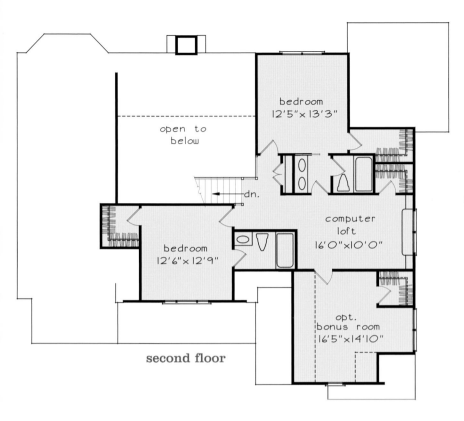

bedroom
12'5"×13'3"

open to
below

dn.

bedroom
12'6"×12'9"

computer
loft
16'0"×10'0"

opt.
bonus room
16'5"×14'10"

second floor

rear elevation

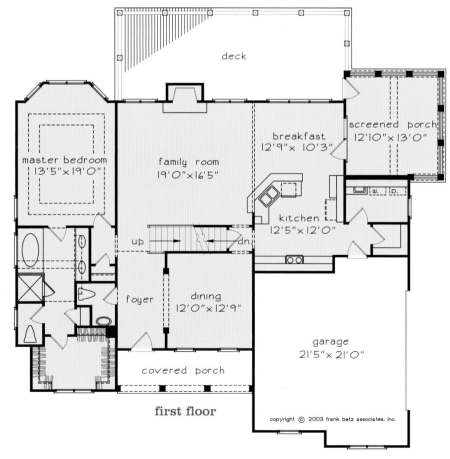

deck

master bedroom
13'5"×19'0"

family room
19'0"×16'5"

breakfast
12'9"× 10'3"

screened porch
12'10"×13'0"

kitchen
12'5"×12'0"

up

dn

foyer

dining
12'0"×12'9"

garage
21'5"×21'0"

covered porch

first floor

Bedrooms: 3

Baths: 3.5

Width: 59'-8"

Depth: 50'-6"

Main Level: 1593 sq ft

Second Level: 796 sq ft

Living Area: 2389 sq ft

Opt. Bonus Room: 238 sq ft

© Frank Betz Associates, Inc.

Ambrose

Designer's Notes

Plan number: CAFB03-3551
PRICE CODE: **E**

A distinctive turret with arched windows is the focal point of the façade on the Ambrose. A covered entry leads to an interesting and thoughtful layout inside. Family time is well spent in the large sunroom, situated just beyond the breakfast area. With its fireplace and built-in cabinetry, this room adds a comfortable and casual element to this home. The bedroom on the main level easily transforms into a home office — perfect for the telecommuter or retiree. An optional bonus room upstairs offers many possibilities for expansion into a children's retreat, craft room or exercise area.

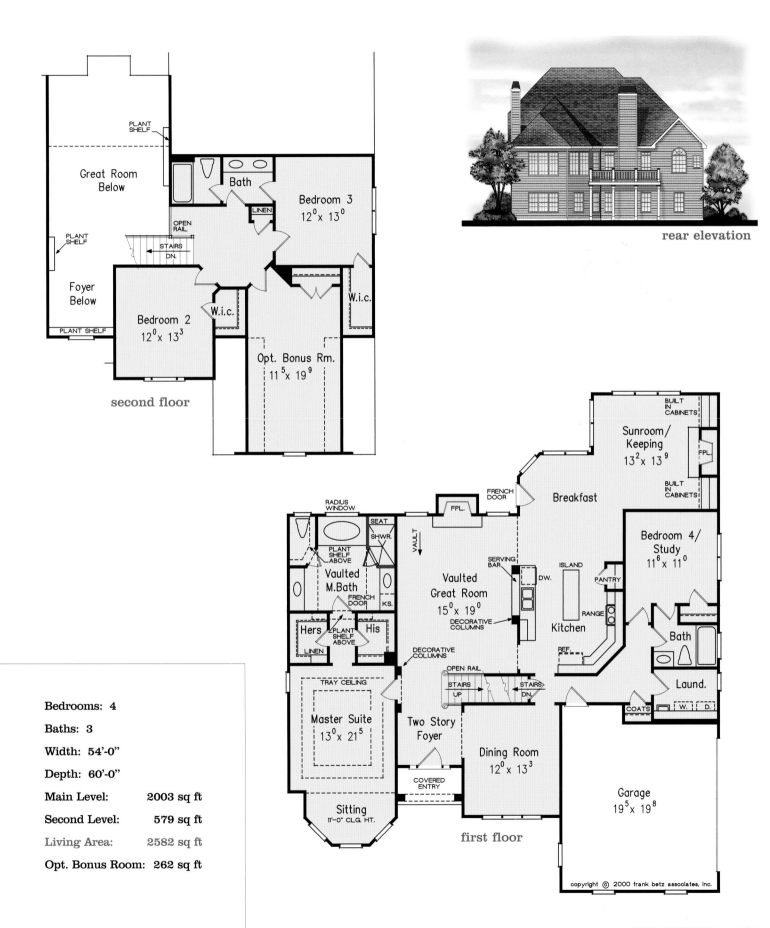

PLANT SHELF

Great Room Below

PLANT SHELF

Foyer Below

PLANT SHELF

Bath

LINEN

Bedroom 3
12⁰ x 13⁰

OPEN RAIL

STAIRS DN.

Bedroom 2
12⁰ x 13³

W.i.c.

W.i.c.

Opt. Bonus Rm.
11⁵ x 19⁹

second floor

rear elevation

RADIUS WINDOW

SEAT
SHWR.

PLANT SHELF ABOVE

Vaulted M.Bath

FRENCH DOOR

KS.

Hers
PLANT SHELF ABOVE
His

LINEN

TRAY CEILING

Master Suite
13⁰ x 21⁵

DECORATIVE COLUMNS

Two Story Foyer

COVERED ENTRY

Sitting
11'-0" CLG. HT.

FPL.

FRENCH DOOR

VAULT

Vaulted Great Room
15⁰ x 19⁰

DECORATIVE COLUMNS

SERVING BAR

DW.

ISLAND

RANGE

PANTRY

REF.

OPEN RAIL

STAIRS UP

STAIRS DN.

Dining Room
12⁰ x 13³

Breakfast

Sunroom/ Keeping
13² x 13⁹

BUILT IN CABINETS

FPL

BUILT IN CABINETS

Bedroom 4/ Study
11⁶ x 11⁰

Kitchen

Bath

Laund.

COATS

W.

D.

Garage
19⁵ x 19⁸

first floor

copyright © 2000 frank betz associates, inc.

Bedrooms: 4

Baths: 3

Width: 54'-0"

Depth: 60'-0"

Main Level: 2003 sq ft

Second Level: 579 sq ft

Living Area: 2582 sq ft

Opt. Bonus Room: 262 sq ft

© Frank Betz Associates, Inc.

Keheley Ridge

Designer's Notes

Plan number: CAFB03-3853
PRICE CODE: **G**

From the Southern Living Design Collection™ – The warm and friendly exterior of the Keheley Ridge was created by combining stone and siding with unique features, such as board-and-batten shutters and carriage doors. This thoughtful grouping creates a façade that has the old world charm that so many homeowners are seeking.

Continuing with this trend of warmth and comfort, a cozy keeping room with a fireplace is situated off the breakfast area. The entertainer will love the butler's pantry that connects the kitchen and dining room. Each bedroom upstairs enjoys the privacy of personal bathing areas. A recreation room is well-positioned on the second floor.

bedroom
14'9"×13'8"

recreation room
17'0"×19'0"

bedroom
13'5"×13'0"

up

bedroom
13'0"×14'10"

dn.

open to
below

second floor

rear elevation

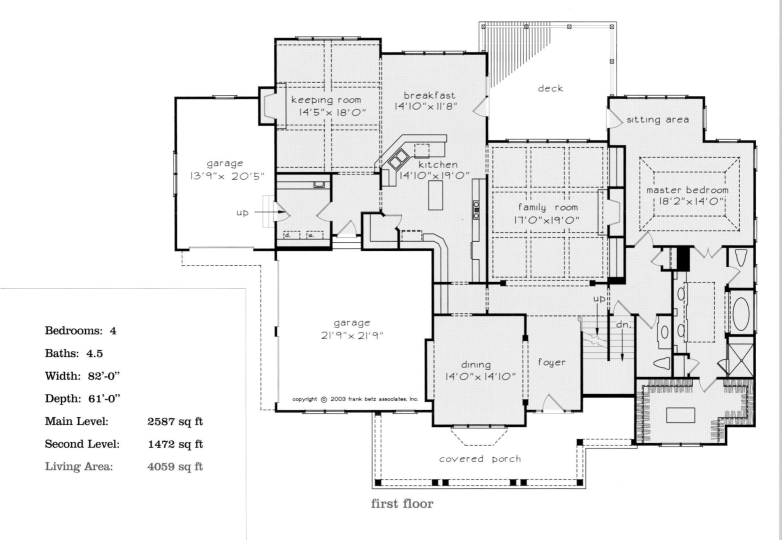

keeping room
14'5"×18'0"

breakfast
14'10"×11'8"

deck

sitting area

garage
13'9"× 20'5"

kitchen
14'10"×19'0"

up

master bedroom
18'2"×14'0"

d. w.

family room
17'0"×19'0"

up

dn.

garage
21'9"× 21'9"

dining
14'0"×14'10"

foyer

copyright © 2003 frank betz associates, inc.

covered porch

first floor

Bedrooms: 4

Baths: 4.5

Width: 82'-0"

Depth: 61'-0"

Main Level: 2587 sq ft

Second Level: 1472 sq ft

Living Area: 4059 sq ft

Holland

Designer's Notes

Plan number: CAFB03-649
PRICE CODE: **B**

First - time homeowners or those seeking to downsize will appreciate the charm and character that the Holland offers in its conservative square footage. A handy serving bar in the kitchen makes casual meal - time and entertaining convenient and fun. The garage entry is routed through the laundry room, keeping shoes and coats in their place.

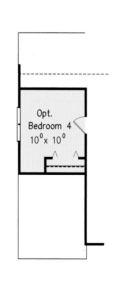

rear elevation

Bedrooms: 4

Baths: 2.5

Width: 41'-0"

Depth: 46'-4"

Main Level: 1144 sq ft

Second Level: 620 sq ft

Living Area: 1764 sq ft

first floor

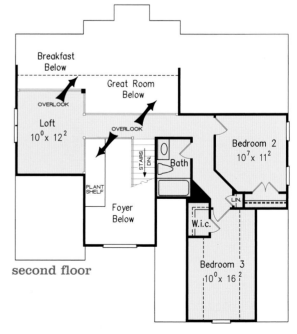

second floor

© Frank Betz Associates, Inc.

rear elevation

Bedrooms: 3

Baths: 2

Width: 56'-4"

Depth: 62'-0"

Main Level: 2057 sq ft

Living Area: 2057 sq ft

Opt. Second Floor: 327 sq ft

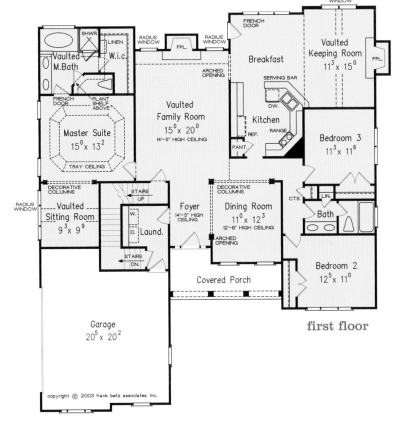

optional second floor

first floor

Seabrooke

Designer's Notes

Plan number: CAFB03-3842
PRICE CODE: **D**

Modern design features inside make this house as family - friendly as it is charming. A vaulted keeping room is situated just off the kitchen area, giving families a comfortable place to spend casual time together. Decorative columns surround the dining room, serving as a subtle divider from the rest of the home.

© Frank Betz Associates, Inc.

Mallory

Designer's Notes

Plan number: CAFB03-992
PRICE CODE: **E**

rear elevation

Everyone knows that family members and guests tend to congregate in the kitchen. The Mallory accommodates this fact, with a vaulted breakfast area and keeping room with fireplace adjoining the kitchen. Two secondary bedrooms — each with a walk-in closet — share a divided bathing area on the second floor. An optional bonus room is ready to finish into a fourth bedroom, playroom or exercise area.

Bedrooms:	3
Baths:	2.5
Width:	54'-0"
Depth:	46'-10"
Main Level:	1628 sq ft
Second Level:	527 sq ft
Living Area:	2155 sq ft
Opt. Bonus Room:	207 sq ft

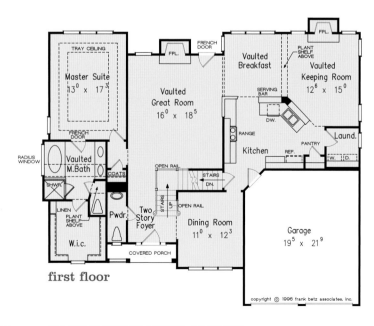

first floor

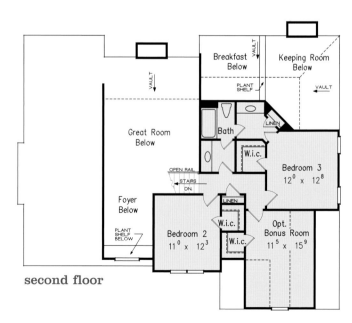

second floor

© Frank Betz Associates, Inc.

Julian

Designer's Notes

Plan number: CAFB03-1262
PRICE CODE: **E**

Homeowners will love the special attention given to the details inside this inviting design. Decorative columns separate the kitchen area from the vaulted family room. Built-in cabinetry and a fireplace make this room a comfortable and charming place to spend time with family and friends. Optional bonus space upstairs leaves plenty of room to grow.

rear elevation

Bedrooms: 3

Baths: 2.5

Width: 53'-0"

Depth: 43'-4"

Main Level:	1626 sq ft
Second Level:	541 sq ft
Living Area:	2167 sq ft
Opt. Bonus Room:	256 sq ft

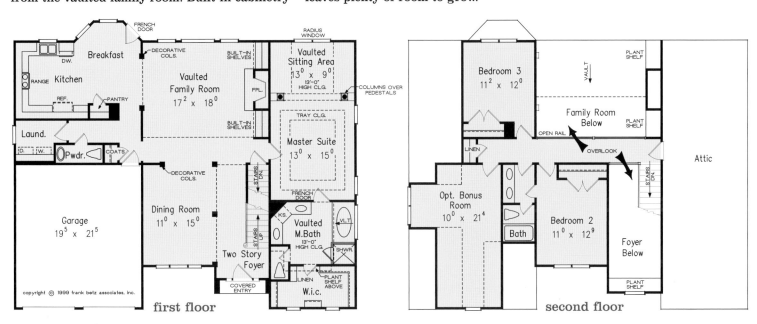

first floor

second floor

© Frank Betz Associates, Inc.

rear elevation

Bedrooms: 4

Baths: 3

Width: 57'-0"

Depth: 62'-4"

Main Level: 1977 sq ft

Second Level: 265 sq ft

Living Area: 2242 sq ft

Mulberry

Designer's Notes

Plan number: CAFB03-3794
PRICE CODE: **D**

Ranch lovers will appreciate the thoughtful and creative design elements incorporated into this brilliant floor plan. A serving bar in the kitchen provides a casual dining spot for informal entertaining and family time. The master suite is extended by a private sitting area that overlooks the backyard, giving homeowners a quiet place of their own to start and end the day.

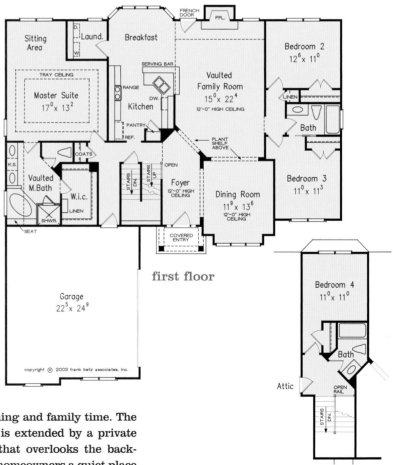

first floor

second floor

© Frank Betz Associates, Inc.

Sullivan

Designer's Notes

Plan number: CAFB03-1224
PRICE CODE: **E**

The Sullivan's full brick façade, as well as the classic turret, has stood the test of time. The home is anchored by a vaulted great room that adjoins the kitchen and breakfast areas – a per- fect layout for entertaining. The master suite is private and well-appointed, complete with his- and-her closets, a lavish bath and comfortable sitting area.

rear elevation

Bedrooms:	4
Baths:	3
Width:	54'-0"
Depth:	48'-0"
Main Level:	1688 sq ft
Second Level:	558 sq ft
Living Area:	2246 sq ft
Opt. Bonus Room:	269 sq ft

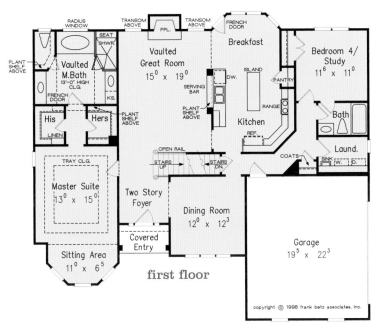

first floor

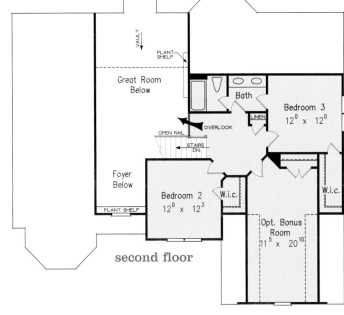

second floor

© Frank Betz Associates, Inc.

rear elevation

Bedrooms: 4

Baths: 3.5

Width: 61'-0"

Depth: 65'-4"

Main Level: 2311 sq ft

Living Area: 2311 sq ft

Opt. Second Floor: 425 sq ft

optional second floor

Opt. Bonus Room 12⁵ x 21⁰

Bath

W.i.c.

STAIRS DN.

first floor

FPL.

Sitting Area

TRAY CLG.

Master Suite 17⁹ x 20⁰

PLANT SHELF ABOVE

VAULT

VAULT VAULT

Vaulted Breakfast

FRENCH DOOR

RADIUS WINDOW

VAULT

Bedroom 2 12² x 11⁶

Bath

RANGE

DW.

PASS THRU

Vaulted Family Room 16⁰ x 22⁶ 15'-0" HIGH CEILING

FPL.

Hers

Kitchen

REF.

PANTRY

LINEN

PLANT SHELF ABOVE

Vaulted M.Bath

K.S.

Bedroom 3 11⁰ x 11⁰

SHWR

His

LINEN

W.D.

Pwdr.

STAIRS UP

ARCHED OPENINGS

PLANT SHELF ABOVE

COATS

Laund.

COATS

Foyer 15'-0" HIGH CEILING

Dining Room 12⁹ x 12⁸ 15'-0" HIGH CEILING

Vaulted Living Room/ Opt. Bedroom 4 12⁵ x 12⁹

STAIRS TO OPT. BSMT.

COVERED PORCH

Garage 22⁵ x 21⁰

copyright © 1996 frank betz associates, inc.

Cassidy

Designer's Notes

Plan number: CAFB03-969

PRICE CODE: **E**

A smart and functional split - bedroom design, the Cassidy is made extra special in its details. The master suite has a private sitting area with a fireplace that gives owners a peaceful place to spend time reading or relaxing. A vaulted ceiling keeps the breakfast room feeling open and bright. Plant shelves and arched openings add touches of character throughout the home.

© Frank Betz Associates, Inc.

Carlton Square

Designer's Notes

Plan number: CAFB03-3588
PRICE CODE: **D**

The entertainer will love the unobstructed design on the main level of the Carlton Square. The kitchen connects with ease to a vaulted keeping room, breakfast area and the grand room, generating effortless traffic flow from one space to the next. Also on the main level, a bedroom can be easily converted into a home office – perfect for teleworkers or retirees.

rear elevation

Bedrooms:	4
Baths:	3
Width:	60'-0"
Depth:	53'-0"
Main Level:	1961 sq ft
Second Level:	520 sq ft
Living Area:	2481 sq ft
Opt. Bonus Room:	265 sq ft

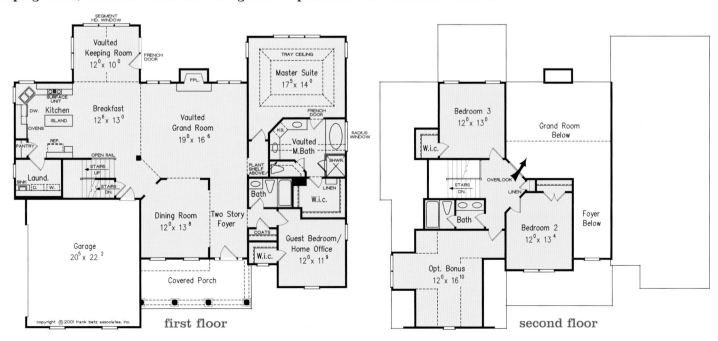

first floor

second floor

© Frank Betz Associates, Inc.

rear elevation

Bedrooms: 4

Baths: 3.5

Width: 63'-0"

Depth: 67'-6"

Main Level: 2548 sq ft

Living Area: 2548 sq ft

Opt. Second Floor: 490 sq ft

Hennefield

Designer's Notes

Plan number: CAFB03-3835
PRICE CODE: **E**

This one-level design is equipped with several added extras that make it original and unique. Just off the kitchen is a vaulted keeping room that is bright and comfortable with radius windows that allow natural light to illuminate the room. Built-in cabinetry in the family room gives this area an appealing focal point, as well as ample storage and decorating opportunities.

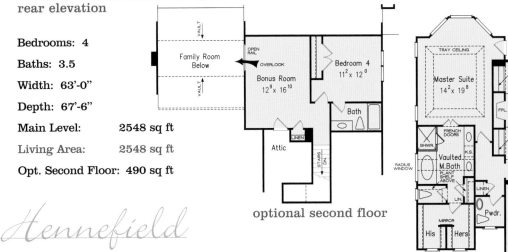

optional second floor

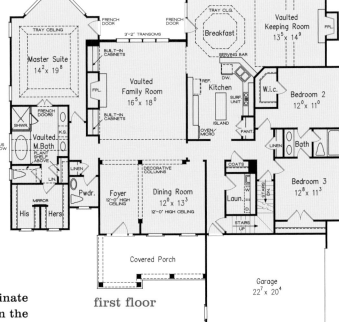

first floor

copyright © 2003 frank betz associates, inc.

© Frank Betz Associates, Inc.

Arramore

Designer's Notes

Plan number: CAFB03-3869
PRICE CODE: **E**

This floor plan is brilliantly designed, using every inch of its 2,792 square feet to offer the latest and greatest amenities offered today. A bright and sunny keeping room is connected to the kitchen and breakfast areas. A coffered ceiling and transom windows make the family room extra special. A children's retreat is included in the upper level of this design, giving kids plenty of space to play.

rear elevation

Bedrooms: 4

Baths: 3

Width: 44'-0"

Depth: 58'-0"

Main Level: 1365 sq ft

Second Level: 1427 sq ft

Living Area: 2792 sq ft

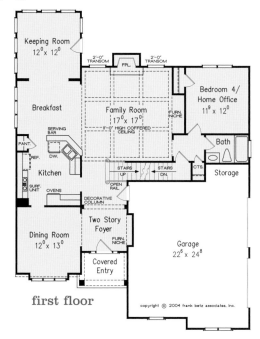

first floor

second floor

copyright © 2004 frank betz associates, inc.

© Frank Betz Associates, Inc.

rear elevation

Bedrooms: 3

Baths: 3.5

Width: 65'-4"

Depth: 85'-6"

Main Level: 2876 sq ft

Living Area: 2876 sq ft

Opt. Second Floor: 393 sq ft

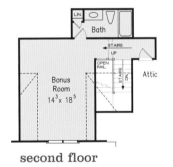

second floor

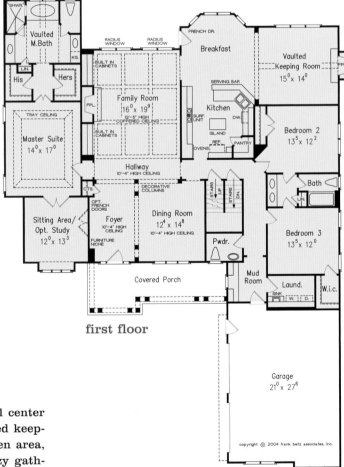

first floor

Stoney River

Designer's Notes

Plan number: CAFB03-3866

PRICE CODE: **E**

The Stoney River's inviting Old World exterior is followed by many unique and special design elements inside. Coffered ceilings and built-in cabinetry in the family room make this room the natural center point of the home. A vaulted keeping room adjoins the kitchen area, providing an additional cozy gathering spot.

© Frank Betz Associates, Inc.

Greenlaw

Designer's Notes

Plan number: CAFB03-3559
PRICE CODE: **F**

The Greenlaw is a wonderful design for today's growing and active family. A vaulted keeping room, breakfast area, kitchen and covered porch come together to create a comfortable core of the home where family and company will likely gather. The home office can be effortlessly converted into a nursery with easy access from the master suite.

rear elevation

Bedrooms: 4

Baths: 4

Width: 64'-0"

Depth: 55'-2"

Main Level: 2247 sq ft

Second Level: 637 sq ft

Living Area: 2884 sq ft

Opt. Bonus Room: 235 sq ft

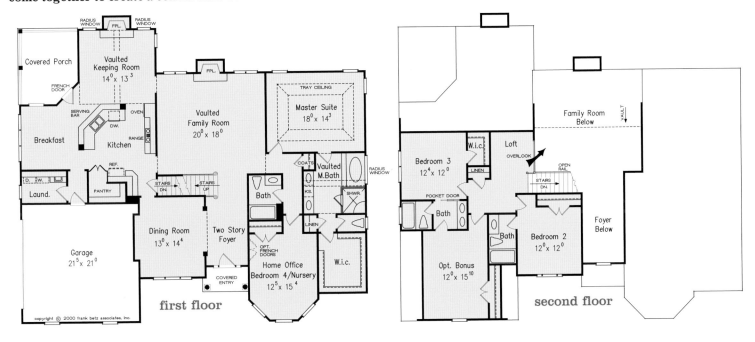

first floor

second floor

© Frank Betz Associates, Inc.

Prescott Ridge

Designer's Notes

Plan number: CAFB03-3746
PRICE CODE: **F**

Original and thoughtful design talent went into every detail of the Prescott Ridge. The well-planned kitchen is complete with a cook-top island and double ovens. A window seat creates the back wall of the keeping room, adding charm and comfort to the room. It shares a two-sided fireplace with the neighboring two-story great room.

rear elevation

Bedrooms:	5
Baths:	4
Width:	59'-0"
Depth:	55'-6"
Main Level:	2052 sq ft
Second Level:	833 sq ft
Living Area:	2885 sq ft

first floor

second floor

Montaigne

Designer's Notes

Plan number: CAFB03-3731
PRICE CODE: **E**

Granite-gray shutters, native stone and shingles create the right mix of rugged and refined elements in this rural Old World classic. A gallery foyer defined by arches and columns grants vistas that extend from the entry to the back property. Bay windows in the breakfast area, master suite and an upper-level bedroom invite a sense of nature throughout the home.

rear elevation

Bedrooms: 4

Baths: 3.5

Width: 62'-4"

Depth: 50'-0"

Main Level: 1897 sq ft

Second Level: 1086 sq ft

Living Area: 2983 sq ft

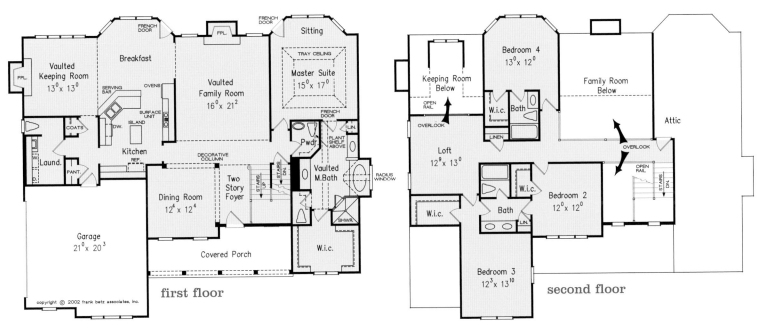

first floor

second floor

© Frank Betz Associates, Inc.

rear elevation

Heyward

Designer's Notes

Plan number: CAFB03-1205
PRICE CODE: **E**

A clean and uncomplicated design, this home is highly functional and accommodating. The kitchen, breakfast area and family room connect to create one gathering spot. The master suite encompasses the entire back of the upper level, with serene views to the backyard from all its vantage points. Laundry facilities are centrally located upstairs, with easy access to all of the bedrooms.

Bedrooms:	5
Baths:	4
Width:	54'-0"
Depth:	42'-4"
Main Level:	1408 sq ft
Second Level:	1598 sq ft
Living Area:	3006 sq ft

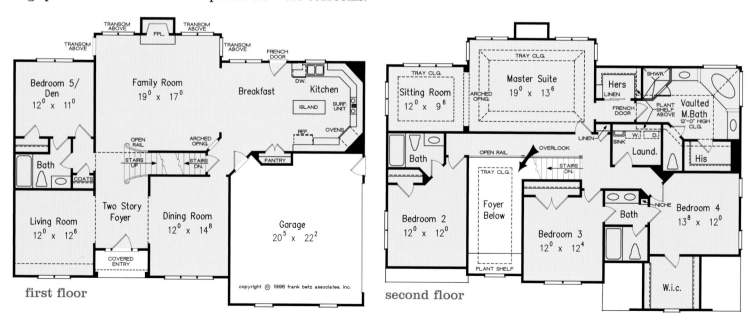

© Frank Betz Associates, Inc.

Burgess

Designer's Notes

Plan number: CAFB03-883
PRICE CODE: **D**

The Burgess sums up the warmth and character that Old World style is known to exude. The formal dining room steps down to a vaulted living room, giving party guests a great place to retreat after dining. A coffered ceiling draws attention to its soaring two-story height.

rear elevation

Bedrooms: 4

Baths: 3.5

Width: 52'-4"

Depth: 55'-4"

Main Level: 1468 sq ft

Second Level: 1559 sq ft

Living Area: 3027 sq ft

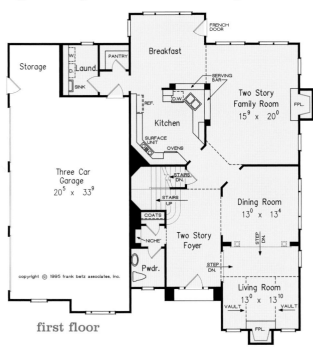

first floor

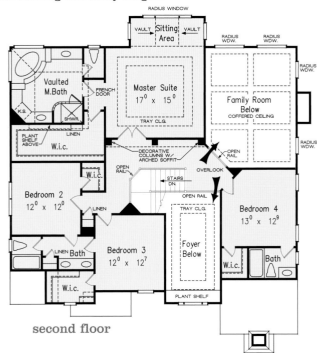

second floor

© Frank Betz Associates, Inc.

Huntcliffe

Designer's Notes

Plan number: CAFB03-844
PRICE CODE: **E**

Unique angles and modern-day design trends inside make this home original and exciting. Even the most discriminating chefs will love this enormous kitchen with a prep island, double ovens, walk-in pantry and built-in message center. It is adjoined by an octagonal breakfast room with a tray ceiling. The family room is situated at a 45 - degree angle, creating an interesting and original main - floor layout.

rear elevation

Bedrooms: 4

Baths: 3.5

Width: 56'-0"

Depth: 47'-6"

Main Level:	1415 sq ft
Second Level:	1632 sq ft
Living Area:	3047 sq ft

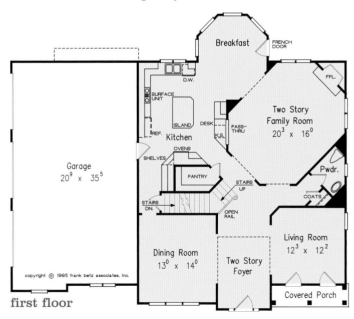

first floor

copyright © 1995 frank betz associates, inc.

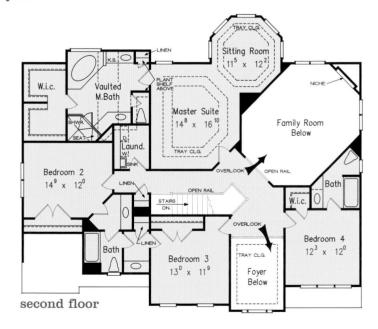

second floor

© Frank Betz Associates, Inc.

Brambleton

Designer's Notes

Plan number: CAFB03-3760
PRICE CODE: **E**

The Brambleton's façade is comprised of board-and-batten siding, brick and copper accents, giving it that informal, yet upscale feeling that is so sought after today. "Keeping" with this charm-ing theme is a casual and cozy keeping room, just off the kitchen, which is complete with double ovens and a walk-in pantry.

rear elevation

Bedrooms: 5

Baths: 4

Width: 57'-4"

Depth: 42'-0"

Main Level:	1471 sq ft
Second Level:	1580 sq ft
Living Area:	3051 sq ft

first floor

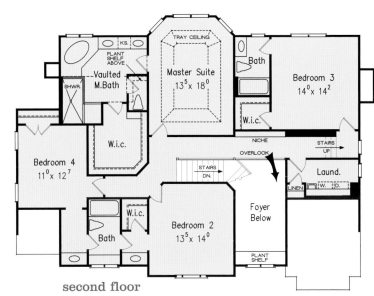

second floor

© Frank Betz Associates, Inc.

rear elevation

Bedrooms: 4

Baths: 3

Width: 65'-4"

Depth: 53'-8"

Main Level: 2224 sq ft

Second Level: 1030 sq ft

Living Area: 3254 sq ft

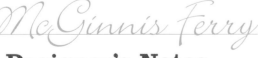
McGinnis Ferry

second floor

first floor

copyright © 2004 frank betz associates, inc.

Designer's Notes

Plan number: CAFB03-3879

PRICE CODE: **E**

Fieldstone accents against board-and-batten siding generate the welcoming and warm appeal that Old World homes are known for. A vaulted keeping room connects to the kitchen and breakfast areas, creating that relaxing place to rest and unwind. A teen suite upstairs is equipped with a built-in desk, making this spot the perfect homework station and recreational hang-out.

© Frank Betz Associates, Inc.

Fenway

Designer's Notes

Plan number: CAFB03-3444
PRICE CODE: **F**

Fieldstone accents with board-and-batten shutters create that warm, cottage-like façade that is so popular today. A fire-lit keeping room borders the kitchen and breakfast area, providing the ideal setting for casual gatherings. Private lounging space has been incorporated into the master suite, giving homeowners a tranquil spot to start and end their days.

rear elevation

Bedrooms: 4

Baths: 3.5

Width: 71'-0"

Depth: 62'-0"

Main Level: 2293 sq ft

Second Level: 992 sq ft

Living Area: 3285 sq ft

Opt. Bonus Room: 131 sq ft

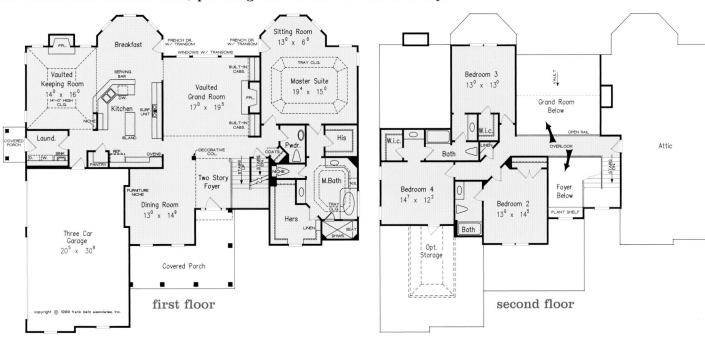

first floor

second floor

© Frank Betz Associates, Inc.

Muirfield

Designer's Notes

Plan number: CAFB03-3769
PRICE CODE: **F**

The Muirfield was designed to cater to the lifestyle of today's growing family. The kitchen, breakfast area and vaulted keeping room create a unified space for casual family time. His-and-

rear elevation

her closets and a lavish master bath create a "suite" spot to start and end your day. A built-in desk in the second-floor loft creates the perfect homework station for kids.

Bedrooms: 4

Baths: 3.5

Width: 72'-0"

Depth: 60'-6"

Main Level: 2153 sq ft

Second Level: 1036 sq ft

Living Area: 3189 sq ft

Opt. Bonus Room: 114 sq ft

© Frank Betz Associates, Inc.

Candace

Designer's Notes

Plan number: CAFB03-965
PRICE CODE: **G**

The many gables that comprise the front elevation of the Candace give it appealing dimension and fantastic curb appeal. Decorative columns and arched openings serve as transitional points from various rooms, adding to the charm and character of this design. An optional bonus room upstairs has endless finishing possibilities, such as a playroom or exercise area.

rear elevation

Bedrooms: 4

Baths: 3.5

Width: 63'-4"

Depth: 57'-0"

Main Level:	2384 sq ft
Second Level:	1050 sq ft
Living Area:	3434 sq ft
Opt. Bonus Room:	228 sq ft

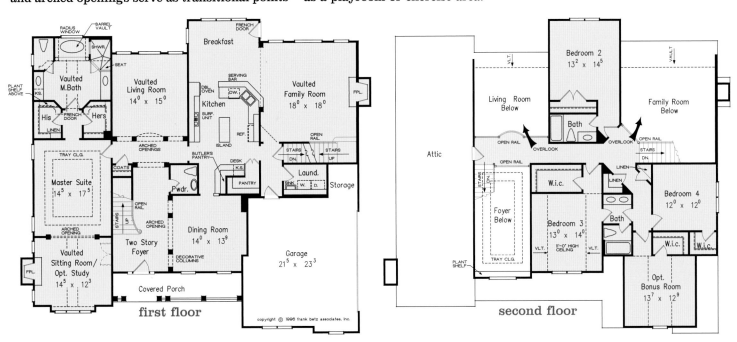

first floor

second floor

copyright © 1996 frank betz associates, inc.

© Frank Betz Associates, Inc.

Witherspoon

Designer's Notes

Plan number: CAFB03-3462
PRICE CODE: **G**

A stone turret gives the Witherspoon the Old World charm that is in high demand today. Distinctive and elegant, tray ceilings enhance the master suite. A seated shower, double sinks and his-and-her closets make for an enviable master bath. Optional bonus space upstairs gives homeowners extra space for a home gym or playroom.

rear elevation

Bedrooms: 5

Baths: 4.5

Width: 64'-6"

Depth: 57'-10"

Main Level: 2384 sq ft

Second Level: 1234 sq ft

Living Area: 3618 sq ft

Opt. Bonus Room: 344 sq ft

first floor

copyright © 1999 frank betz associates, inc.

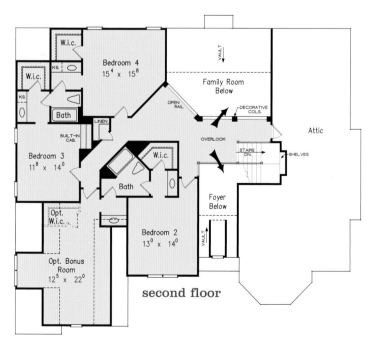

second floor

© Frank Betz Associates, Inc.

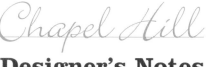

rear elevation

Bedrooms: 5

Baths: 4.5

Width: 69'-0"

Depth: 79'-0"

Main Level:	2727 sq ft
Second Level:	981 sq ft
Living Area:	3708 sq ft

Chapel Hill

Designer's Notes

Plan number: CAFB03-3872
PRICE CODE: **F**

The Chapel Hill's main floor features two master suites – a rare find in home plans today. A roomy and well-appointed kitchen is adjoined by a cozy keeping room. Its fireplace, built-in cabinetry and transom windows make this a comfortable and casual gathering spot for the whole family.

second floor

first floor

© Frank Betz Associates, Inc.

rear elevation

second floor

Bedrooms: 4

Baths: 3.5

Width: 79'-0"

Depth: 73'-4"

Main Level: 2269 sq ft

Second Level: 1551 sq ft

Living Area: 3820 sq ft

Wedgewood

Designer's Notes

Plan number: CAFB03-3887
PRICE CODE: **F**

The Wedgewood was crafted with today's busy and growing family in mind. A vaulted keeping room is situated off the kitchen area, giving families a comfortable and casual place to spend their time. The master suite is the only bedroom on the main level, ensuring a sense of privacy and peacefulness. A children's den is incorporated into the upper level, making an ideal playroom. Each bedroom upstairs has direct access to a bath.

first floor

Hartford Springs

Designer's Notes

Plan number: CAFB03-3824
PRICE CODE: **G**

From the Southern Living Design Collection™ – Thoughtful details are what make Hartford Springs a unique and well-designed home. Two decks are situated on the back of the home: a handy grilling porch located off the

rear elevation

kitchen, as well as a full-sized sunning deck. A fireplace creates cozy family time spent in the vaulted keeping room. A spacious teen suite easily converts into a playroom or homework station.

Bedrooms: 4

Baths: 3.5

Width: 73'-0"

Depth: 66'-10"

Main Level:	2504 sq ft
Second Level:	1467 sq ft
Living Area:	3971 sq ft

first floor

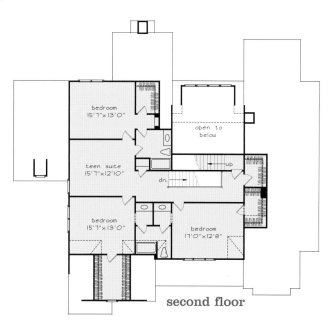

second floor

© Frank Betz Associates, Inc.

rear elevation

Castlegate

Designer's Notes

Plan number: CAFB03-790
PRICE CODE: **G**

A portico entry leads into a breathtaking two-story foyer with a curved staircase. The master suite is appropriately named, with its vaulted sitting room and luxurious bath. The kitchen is equipped with every creature comfort imaginable, such as an island with a surface unit and serving bar, double ovens and a butler's pantry.

Bedrooms: 4
Baths: 3.5
Width: 74'-6"
Depth: 65'-10"
Main Level: 2764 sq ft
Second Level: 1598 sq ft
Living Area: 4362 sq ft

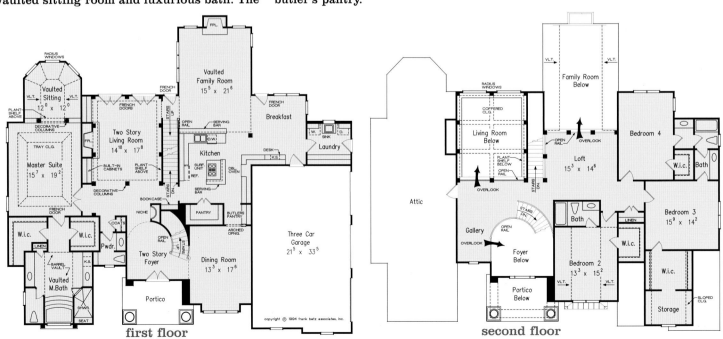

first floor

second floor

copyright © 1994 frank betz associates, inc.

Castlegate White architectural columns soar nearly two stories to uphold a grand covered entry, graced by ornate French doors.

Top | Combining floral with plaid brings a casual elegance to this family room.

Above | Built - in cabinetry adds a decorative element to the dining room, giving homeowners a place to personalize their space with family photos and memorabilia.

OLD WORLD   153

Plan Index

† Indicates photographed homes not featured in Homes With Curb Appeal. Please visit www.homeswithcurbappeal.com to view full plan details.

Construction Drawing
Information

CONSTRUCTION DRAWINGS

Each set of plans from Frank Betz Associates, Inc., will provide you with the necessary information needed to construct a home. The actual number of pages may vary, but each set of plans will contain the following information:

1 FRONT ELEVATIONS/DETAILS

All plans include the front elevation at 1/4" or 3/16" scale and the sides and rear elevations at 1/8" scale. The elevations show and note the exterior finished materials of the house.

2 ELEVATIONS/ROOF PLAN

The side and rear elevations are shown at 1/8" scale. The roof plan is a "bird's eye" view, showing the roof pitches, overhangs, ridges, valleys and any saddles.

3 FOUNDATION PLAN

Every plan is available with a walk-out style basement (three masonry walls and one wood-framed rear wall with windows and doors). The basement plans are a 1/4" scale layout of unfinished spaces showing only the necessary 2 x 6 wood-framed load-bearing walls. Crawl foundations and/or slab-on-grade foundations are available for many plans. All foundation types are not available for all plans.

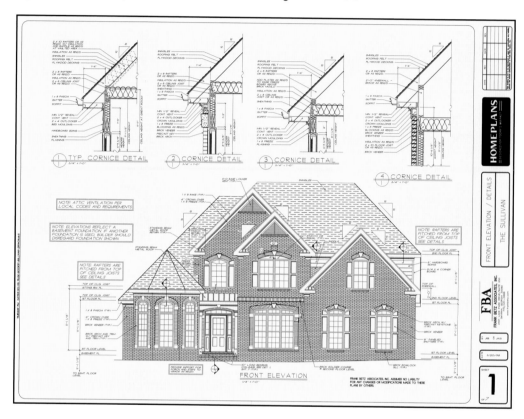

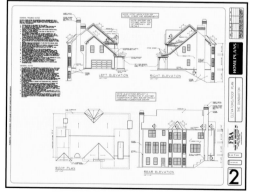

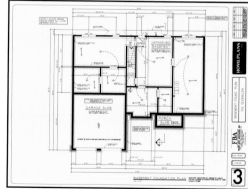

4 FLOOR PLANS

Each plan consists of 1/4" or 3/16" scale floor layouts showing the location of walls, doors, windows, plumbing fixtures, cabinetry, stairs and decorative ceilings. The floor plans are complete with dimensions, notes, door/window sizes and schematic electrical layout.

5 SECTION(S)

The building sections are drawings which take vertical cuts through the house and stairs showing floor, ceiling and roof height information.

6 KITCHEN AND BATH ELEVATIONS/DETAILS

The kitchen and bath elevations show the arrangement and size of each cabinet and other fixtures in the room. These drawings give basic information that can be used to create customized layouts with a cabinet manufacturer. Details are included for many interior and exterior conditions to provide more specific construction information.

7 FIRST AND SECOND FLOOR FRAMING PLANS

The floor - framing plans show each floor joist indicating the size, spacing and length. All beams are labeled and sized. All of the joists are counted and coordinated with the material list. Each framing plan sheet includes any framing details that are needed (tray details, connection details, etc.). The framing plans are designed using conventional framing (2 x 8, 2 x 10) or wood I-Joists, depending on the span conditions of each individual design.

8 CEILING JOIST FRAMING

The ceiling - joist framing plan shows each ceiling joist indicating the size, spacing and length. All beams are labeled and sized. All of the joists are counted and coordinated with the material list.

9 ROOF FRAMING PLAN

The roof - framing plan shows each rafter, valley, hip and ridge indicating the size, spacing and length. All beams are labeled and sized. All of the joists are counted and coordinated with the material list.

TYPICAL DETAIL SHEETS

Each plan order includes one set of typical detail sheets that show foundation details, typical wall sections and other framing details. Also included on the detail sheets are miscellaneous interior trim and fireplace details that can be used to customize the home.

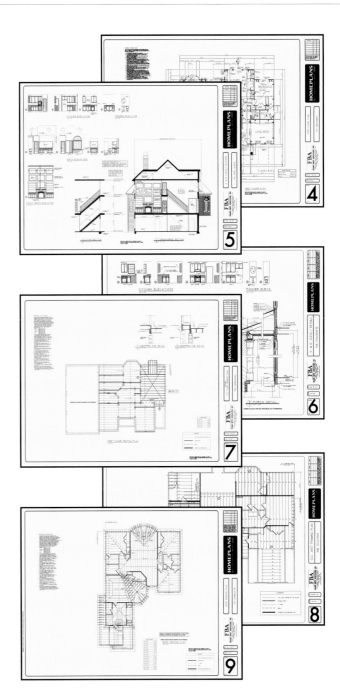

Ordering
Information

PRICING INFORMATION

Pricing information for our plans can be found in the Plan Index (pages 154-155) and on the Order Form (page 159). Pricing for additional products can also be found on the Order Form. Pricing and plan set information are subject to change without notice.

SHIPPING INFORMATION

Typically, we ship our orders the following business day after receipt of order. All plans are shipped via Federal Express 2-day or Overnight. Plans must be shipped to a street address as Federal Express will not deliver to a Post Office Box.

OUR EXCHANGE POLICY

Plans may be returned for a full refund, less applicable restocking fees and shipping charges, by returning the **unopened** package to our office. No returns will be accepted on open boxes, electronic CAD files, or electronic or printed artwork. Plans may be exchanged within 30 days of purchase. Exchanges are subject to price difference and restocking fees.

CODE COMPLIANCE

Our plans are drawn to meet the 2000 International Residential Code for One and Two Family Dwellings and the 2000 International Building Code with the Georgia Amendments. Many states and counties amend the code for their area. Each building department's requirements for a permit may vary. Consult your local building officials to determine the plan, code and site requirements. Frank Betz Associates Homeplans are not stamped by an architect or engineer. Our plans include the drawings typically needed for construction, except site-specific information and heating and cooling requirements. This information, if required, must be provided based on the geographic conditions in your area.

HOW TO ORDER

When placing an order, you may do so online, by mail, fax or phone. To order online, visit www.homeswithcurbappeal.com and follow the directions to the order form. To speak to a customer service representative call 888-717-3003. Orders may be faxed to 770-435-7608 or mailed to Betz Publishing, 2401 Lake Park Drive, Suite 250, Smyrna, Georgia 30080. We accept Visa, Mastercard, American Express and Discover. Orders can also be sent COD for an additional charge. COD orders require certified funds!

IGNORING COPYRIGHT LAWS
CAN BE AN EXPENSIVE MISTAKE

Recent changes in the US copyright laws allow for statutory damages of up to $150,000.00 per incident for copyright infringement involving any of the copyrighted plans found in this publication. The law can be confusing. So, for your own protection, take the time to understand what you can and cannot do when it comes to house plans. Please call us for more information on copyright laws.

Order Form

BETZ PUBLISHING LLC.
2401 Lake Park Drive, Suite 250
Smyrna, GA 30080
1.888.717.3003 | **www.homeswithcurbappeal.com**

PLAN PRICES*

CODE	8 SETS	REPRODUCIBLE	CAD
A	$ 645.00	$ 720.00	$ 1145.00
B	$ 705.00	$ 780.00	$ 1245.00
C	$ 765.00	$ 840.00	$ 1345.00
D	$ 825.00	$ 900.00	$ 1445.00
E	$ 885.00	$ 960.00	$ 1545.00
F	$ 945.00	$1020.00	$ 1645.00
G	$1005.00	$1080.00	$ 1745.00

*Prices subject to change without notice

ADDITIONAL PRODUCTS

Additional Sets . . . .$ 45.00

Additional Foundations*
   slab . . . .$ 125.00
   basement and crawl . . . .$ 175.00
       *All foundations are not available for all plans.

Material Workbooks . . . .$ 85.00

Camera-Ready Artwork
   11″ x 17″ – Color . . . .$ 125.00
   8.5″ x 11″ – Color . . . .$ 75.00
   8.5″ x 11″ – Black and White . . . .$ 50.00

SHIPPING

Federal Express 2-Day . . . .$ 25.00

Federal Express Overnight . . . .$ 40.00

C.O.D. (certified funds required) . . . .$ 15.00

For International shipping, please call our office.

ORDER FORM

PLAN NUMBER _____

SETS NEEDED

☐ 8 - Set Package . . . .$ _____

_____ Number of Sets Reversed

☐ Reproducible . . . .$ _____

☐ CAD . . . .$ _____

☐ Additional Sets @ $ 45.00 each . . . .$ _____

☐ Material Workbook @ $ 85.00 . . . .$ _____

Sub Total _____

Shipping _____

C.O.D. add $ 15.00 _____

Total _____

PAYMENT TYPE (check one)

☐ Visa ☐ Mastercard ☐ American Express ☐ Discover

Credit Card Number_____

Expiration Date_____

Signature _____

Name _____

Company_____

Street_____

City_____ State _____ Zip _____

Daytime Telephone Number _____

Email Address _____

Acknowledgements

For each of us, our idea of home is different. Some want a more formal home, while others want something that evokes a warm comfortable feeling. The homes and plans in this issue give the readers a choice. The curb appeal of a home is what defines it. It welcomes our family and friends. The builders and homeowners who have graciously allowed us to photograph the homes in this book are owed a debt of gratitude. They took our vision and made it a reality. Special thanks to: Whittemore Homes, DMD Associates, JL Brooks Construction, Cooper Homes, Home Traditions, Homes of Cornerstone, Ken Walker, Lone Star Custom Homes, Inc., Carey and Tammy Elam and Alan and Linda Cantrell.

Homes with Curb Appeal